The Book of Football Quotations

THE BOOK OF
Football
Quotations

Peter Ball and Phil Shaw

STANLEY PAUL

LONDON   SYDNEY   AUCKLAND   JOHANNESBURG

Stanley Paul and Co. Ltd
An imprint of Century Hutchinson
Brookmount House, 62–65 Chandos Place,
Covent Garden, London WC2N 4NW

Century Hutchinson Australia (Pty) Ltd
20 Alfred Street, Milson's Point, Sydney 2061

Century Hutchinson New Zealand Limited
191 Archers Road, PO Box 40–086, Glenfield, Auckland 10

Century Hutchinson South Africa (Pty) Ltd
PO Box 337, Bergvlei 2012, South Africa

First published 1984
Reprinted 1984
Revised edition 1986
Second revised edition 1989
Reprinted 1990
Reprinted 1991

Copyright © Peter Ball and Phil Shaw 1984, 1986, 1989
Set in Linotron Times by Deltatype Ltd, Ellesmere Port, Cheshire

Printed and bound in Great Britain by
Mackays of Chatham PLC, Chatham, Kent

British Library Cataloguing in Publication Data
The Book of football quotations. – New ed.
1. Association football. Quotations
I. Ball, Peter, 1943 – II. Shaw, Phil 796.334

ISBN 0 09 174057 6

Contents

Acknowledgements

This book, now in its third edition, would not have existed without the efforts, albeit often unwitting, of hundreds of others.

Our first thanks are to the players, managers, officials and fans who made it all possible, and especially to the journalists who waited in the rain at Tottenham, the street at West Brom, or (at least under cover) in the crowded corridor at Anfield to record their 'nanny goats'. They are too numerous to mention by name, but every reporter for the popular and local press can take our gratitude as read.

We are indebted for their contributions and suggestions to Patrick Barclay, Charles Burgess, Peter Corrigan, Joe and Bill Davies, Eamon Dunphy, Fred Eyre, Brian Glanville, Geoffrey Green, Stan Hey, Frank Keating, Simon Kelner, David Lacey, David Miller, Barry Purchese, Ian Ridley, John Roberts, Russell Thomas and Andy Ward.

David Barber of the Football Association deserves special thanks for guiding us through the FA library, while Neil Morton and his fellow quote-collectors on the *Independent*'s sports desk have been a terrific source of material and encouragement.

Sarah Ball, still living with wall-to-wall newspapers after all these years (since we began compiling quotes for *Time Out* in the mid-1970s) again tolerated the enterprise with remarkable good humour. Julie Shaw has also learned uncomplainingly to share a house with tons of newsprint, scissors and paste. And the enthusiasm of Roddy Bloomfield and Marion Paull made us delighted Stanley Paul were our publishers.

Peter Ball and Phil Shaw

June 1989

1

The Greats and Others

Players

John Aldridge

I see Aldridge has kept a clean sheet again.

JOURNALIST in Windsor Park press-box after Liverpool striker's 19th goalless game for the Republic of Ireland, **1988**.

HE's a good penalty-taker. I'll give him that. As good as any I've seen. But I wouldn't have bought him.

BOB PAISLEY, ex-Liverpool manager, a month before FA Cup final, **1988**.

I wish I were dead. I've never felt so bad in my life. I felt like dying because I had let so many people down – the people of Liverpool, who I love.

ALDRIDGE after missing a penalty in the 1–0 Cup final defeat by Wimbledon, **1988**.

Ossie Ardiles

THEY can't expect to come here and play like fancy flickers. They've joined the toughest league in the world and they'll have to take the knocks. That tackle was to make it clear to him that he wasn't just playing against a Third Division side. It was to say 'This is a man's league' – and he didn't like it. I think Spurs ought to buy a good stock of cotton wool for such posers. They can't expect not to be tackled just because Argentina won the World Cup.

TOMMY SMITH, former Liverpool hard man, after Swansea *v* Spurs League Cup tie, **1978**.

TOMMY very nice man, very nice player.

ARDILES.

HE was everywhere. It was like trying to tackle dust.

JOE ROYLE, Oldham manager, **1988**.

I can't repeat what I said to him, but I had to call heavily on my Spanish.

JIM SMITH, Queen's Park Rangers manager, after Ardiles had given away a late equaliser, **1988**.

Alan Ball

I taught football to him not as a game, but as a way of life.

ALAN BALL SENIOR on his son, **1972**.

Gordon Banks

AT that moment I hated Gordon Banks more than any man in soccer. But when I cooled down I had to applaud him with my heart. It was the greatest save I had ever seen.

PELE after Brazil *v* England, Guadalajara, World Cup, **1970**.

John Barnes

HAVING a priest cane him every weekend . . . I thought: 'That'll be good for him.'

COLONEL KEN BARNES on his son's upbringing, **1988**.

I sat there and heard guys in the stand say, 'Where the devil did he come from?' I bit my tongue.

TERRY BATCHELOR, who tipped off Watford about Barnes, recalling his debut, **1988**.

HE was criticised at Watford for turning it on only in big games. At Liverpool every game is big.

ALAN HANSEN, Liverpool captain, **1988**.

THAT Barnes lad can play!

TOMMY SMITH, finally won over in February **1988**.

HE could turn us over, no bother . . . if he does, I'll kill him.

GRAHAM TAYLOR, Aston Villa manager and Barnes's Watford mentor, **1988**.

As the ball came over I remembered what Graham Taylor said about my having no right foot – so I headed it in.

BARNES on scoring for Liverpool against Villa in the FA Cup, **1988**.

HE'S so relaxed, polite and charming to everybody. Nothing upsets him for long. And he is just as laid back about his food. I've never seen a better eater . . . Indian, Chinese, Mexican. You serve it and Digger will see it off.

PETER BEARDSLEY, Liverpool and England colleague, **1988**.

Jim Baxter

IN the last minute, with the game won, he took the ball from the Rapid penalty area back towards his own goal, as the Viennese gaped, and when still untackled went back down the left wing with it. Then Walter Skocik went in from behind and Baxter went down. A leg was broken. Typically he said, 'I overdid it.'

JOHN RAFFERTY, soccer journalist, on the Rapid v Rangers match, 1964, in *One Hundred Years of Scottish Football*, **1973**.

Peter Beardsley

THE bottom line is that Beardsley comes from God.

ANDY ROXBURGH, Scotland manager, after the Liverpool player's winner for England, **1988**.

MY entire flat would fit into Beardsley's front room.

VINNY JONES, Wimbledon midfielder, **1988**.

Dave Beasant

(HE) may well be the most influential goalkeeper in the history of the game. As a 'keeper he is one of the best in the First Division; as a long, accurate kicker he supplies the bulk of Wimbledon's approach play. This is a bizarre fact but Beasant doesn't draw up the tactics. He simply makes them work.

JOHN GILES, ex-Leeds and Republic of Ireland player, **1988**.

Franz Beckenbauer

I played golf today the way Franz Beckenbauer played football for West Germany. Close to perfect.

SEVERIANO BALLESTEROS, on winning the German Open, **1988**.

Colin Bell

HE didn't seem to grasp his own freakish strength. . . . I said to him, 'You are a great header of the ball. You have a terrific shot – and you're the best, most powerful runner in the business. Every time you walk off the pitch unable to say that you were streets ahead of the other twenty-one players, you have failed.'

MALCOLM ALLISON, Bell's manager at Manchester City, **1960s**.

George Best

THERE are times when you want to wring his neck. He hangs on to the ball when other players have found better positions. Then out of the blue he does something which wins the match. Then you know you're in the presence of someone special.

PAT CRERAND, Manchester United team-mate, in David Meek, *Anatomy of a Football Star: George Best*, **1970**.

BASICALLY, Best makes a greater appeal to the senses than the other two [Finney and Matthews]. His movements are quicker, lighter, more balletic. He offers the greater surprise to the mind and eye . . . he has the more refined, unexpected range. And with it all, there is his utter disregard of physical danger. . . . He has ice in his veins, warmth in his heart, and timing and balance in his feet.

DANNY BLANCHFLOWER, former Spurs and Northern Ireland captain, as above.

IN six years he has become a cult for youth, a new folk hero, a living James Dean who is a rebel with a cause.

GEOFFREY GREEN, journalist, as above.

THE fellow is a football freak. I don't think of him as a small man. I only see those beautiful, tapering muscles and that magnificent style.

JOE MERCER, former Manchester City manager, as above.

'EL Beatle'.

PORTUGUESE newspaper tribute after Benfica 1, Manchester United 5, **1966**.

I was able to stay in my natural environment and develop there as a respected member of the community. If I had been fifteen years old and pulled off the streets of Belfast onto the pitch at Old Trafford, I feel I'd have ended up as George Best has.

BARRY JOHN, Welsh Rugby Union international, **1972**.

WELL, he's got a drink problem, hasn't he?

DON MEGSON, Bournemouth manager, on why Best was left out of his team, **1983**.

I don't care if he's George Best or Pele. Unless he's willing to do hard training, he won't get a look in.

MALCOLM HOLMAN, Ford Open Prison coach, on Best's arrival, **1985**.

As recently as the late Seventies, to woo our top players home, the authorities introduced all-day drinking in Scottish pubs, a valiant effort that succeeded only in enticing George Best to Hibs.

ONLY AN EXCUSE, BBC Radio Scotland spoof documentary, **1986**.

I live in hope that one day I'll go along to a youth match, as in 1963, watch an unknown youngster for just five minutes and find myself asking: 'My God, who *is* that?'

PAT CRERAND, **1987**.

WE had our problems with the wee feller, but I prefer to remember his genius.

SIR MATT BUSBY, former Manchester United manager, **1988**.

Danny Blanchflower

IN nine matches out of ten, Blanchflower has the ball more than any two other players on the field – it's an expression of his tremendous ego which is just what a great captain needs.

ARTHUR ROWE, Tottenham manager during 'push-and-run' era of 1950s, in Julian Holland, *Spurs – The Double*, **1961**.

A man and all he believed in was on trial on White Hart Lane's heavy, grassless, March mud-heap. Apart from a single unsuccessful sortie at inside-right, Blanchflower had not been seen in a League match since the previous Christmas. But he played that March day with all the grace and culture that he knew. His every move was positive and constructive and filled with the arts of the game. He disregarded the mud and the slippery ball. He ignored the anxiety of two teams fighting relegation and lifted them up to his own high level.

JULIAN HOLLAND, *Spurs – The Double*, **1961**, on Blanchflower's return to the side in 1959 match *v* Leicester, after being dropped and asking for a transfer in January.

IN a poor side Danny is an expensive luxury. That's why I dropped him when we had a poor team. But in a good side as Spurs are now he is a wonderful asset through his unorthodox approach and wonderful ball skill.

BILL NICHOLSON, Spurs' 'double' team manager in **1961**.

Billy Bonds

IF anyone kicked me I used to give Bill a wink and say 'Bonzo! Have you seen what they're doing to me?' Then Bill would sort them out in the next five minutes and I'd have the freedom of the midfield.

TREVOR BROOKING, former West Ham and England midfielder, in *100 Great British Footballers*, **1988**.

Stan Bowles

IF Stan Bowles could pass a betting shop like he can pass a ball he'd have no worries at all.

ERNIE TAGG, Crewe manager who rescued Bowles's career after a free transfer from Bury, in **1974**.

Ian Bowyer

HE's almost a friend.

BRIAN CLOUGH on his captain at Nottingham Forest, **1986**.

Billy Bremner

WHEN he makes an easy pass he has his hands flung wide, a theatrical intensity. The crowd think he is posturing, call him 'big head'. In fact, by his balance and concentration he is ensuring absolute accuracy when so many others are too casual over the undemanding.

ARTHUR ROWE, former Spurs manager, in Tony Pawson, *The Football Managers*, **1973**.

I'M no angel, but I've never kicked anyone deliberately.

BREMNER, **1967**.

Trevor Brooking

TREVOR Brooking floats like a butterfly . . . and stings like one. I have never had a high opinion of him as a player. He has been lucky enough to become a member of teams that he shouldn't really have had a sniff at. I believe his lack of application and that of other players like him have meant relegation for West Ham in the past and the failure to win promotion this time.

BRIAN CLOUGH before **1981** FA Cup final. Brooking, whom Clough once tried to buy for Derby, scored the winning goal.

Steve Bull

PEOPLE say his first touch isn't good, but he usually scores with his second.

GRAHAM TURNER, Wolves manager, **1988**.

RAW, but maybe he will turn out to be a Gerd Muller.

BOBBY ROBSON, England manager, **1989**. Muller scored 62 goals in 68 games for West Germany.

HE has a tremendous presence. As soon as he steps on the field you can sense him thinking, 'How many goals am I going to get today?' You get the impression he just loves seeing the net ripple – that it's an obsession.

PHIL NEAL, Bolton player-manager, **1989**.

FAVOURITE food: conkers in gravy.

BULL 'PROFILE' in *The Memoirs of Seth Bottomley* (Port Vale fanzine), **1989**.

Terry Butcher

I was misled. (He) is not the best centre-half in Britain – he is the best in the world. Technically, he would waltz through any European league and he has a left foot that I would put up against the best. Add to that his aggression and this man is some player.

GRAEME SOUNESS on his Rangers captain in updated *No Half Measures*, **1987**.

HE has a low flashpoint, but that's what makes him a special player.

BOBBY ROBSON, **1988**.

Raich Carter

I played with him for years, but I still don't know how good he was. You can only judge a man as a passer when you've seen him under pressure, and I never saw Raich under pressure. He carried empty space around with him like an umbrella.

WILLIE WATSON, Sunderland and England colleague of **1940s**.

John Charles

EVERYTHING John does is automatic. When he moves into position for a goal chance it is instinctive. Watch me and you will see I am seconds late. I do not possess this intuitiveness – I have to work it all out up here [his head]. I work at the skills as hard as I can. But all my thinking has to be done in my head. My feet do not do my thinking for me as they do for a player like John Charles. That is why I can never be as great a footballer as he.

DANNY BLANCHFLOWER in Julian Holland, *Spurs – The Double*, **1961**.

CHARLES, whom I regard purely and simply as a centre-forward, is not yet in the same class as Tommy Lawton, di Stefano or Dixie Dean. Many good judges think that centre-half is his true position. For me, his tackling does not carry enough 'bite' for a key defender. . . . He does not make enough use of his tremendous physical attributes. Instead, I feel, he likes to play football without bodily contact, which is patently impossible.

STAN CULLIS, Wolves manager of the 1950s, in *All for the Wolves*, **1960**.

Bobby Charlton

THE fact that they accused Bobby Charlton of sheltering me while I 'stole' a bracelet proves I'm innocent. Bobby has never done a dishonest thing in his life.

BOBBY MOORE on the 'jewel theft' incident in Bogota, **1970**.

THAT was a great day. Bobby Charlton nearly bought a drink.

EAMON O'KEEFE recalling his hat-trick which brought Wigan promotion in **1982**. Charlton was a Wigan director.

Allan Clarke

GREAVES was the best of the lot, and certainly in a class of his own in being able to dribble round people, as if they weren't there, to create his own chances. But when it came to actual finishing I'd say Allan was definitely on a par with him. When we had shooting practice at Leicester there were days when I felt almost unbeatable, but Clarkey was probably the only player there who would never be psyched by me. He'd be coming through with the ball and as he hit it, he'd look up as if to say: 'You bloody save that one then.'

PETER SHILTON in Jason Tomas, *The Magnificent Obsession*, **1982**.

Nigel Clough

HE is not just a basic centre-forward. He can unlock a defence not so much by a dribble but with a cunning pass, an intelligently weighted short pass. That's a bit of a lost art among British strikers.

DAVE SEXTON, England Under-21 manager, **1988**.

George Cohen

WE used to say about George Cohen: 'He's hit more photographers than Frank Sinatra.' George was quick and broke up the flanks exceptionally well, but his final ball was rarely on target. Usually he would hit his cross into the crowd, or into the photographers.

BOBBY ROBSON in *Time on the Grass*, **1982**.

Eddie Colman

Sharp as a needle, a brilliant little player. To be honest, I fancied him more than Duncan Edwards.

JOE MERCER, former First Division manager, **1983**.

When he waggled his hips he made the stanchions in the grandstand sway.

HARRY GREGG, Manchester United goalkeeper at **1958** Munich air crash, where 'Snakehips' Colman died.

Charlie Cooke

That Cookie. When he sold you a dummy, you had to pay to get back into the ground.

JIM BAXTER, a Scotland team-mate in **1966–67**.

Johan Cruyff

He has shown how far ahead of his time di Stefano was 20 years ago. In many ways they're identical. They operate over the whole length of the pitch, starting attacks yet being there to help conclude them. Cruyff has the same even temperament as di Stefano, but can be hard, and brave when necessary. A super player.

DETTMAR CRAMER, leading German coach, after **1974** World Cup finals.

Kenny Dalglish

Och, just let him on the park.

JOCK STEIN on whether Dalglish's best position was in attack or midfield, **1978**.

Kenny calls all his goals 'tap-ins' until we come to the end of the season and we are talking money. Suddenly he changes his mind.

BOB PAISLEY, **1982**.

THE best player this club has signed this century.

JOHN SMITH, Liverpool chairman, **1986**.

I never saw anyone in this country to touch him. I can think of only two who could go ahead of him – Pele and possibly Cruyff.

GRAEME SOUNESS, former Liverpool and Scotland team-mate, **1988**.

KENNY was even quiet in the Liverpool team talks – or at least those team talks when the gaffer was there. He would have opinions – strong opinions, but he wouldn't offer them unless asked. But it was a different Kenny when the players were talking about conditions or whatever. In those meetings he came on like a real Govan shipyard shop steward.

SOUNESS, **1988**.

Mark Dennis

I'M sure he'll make it 12 before he finishes.

JIM SMITH, Queen's Park Rangers manager, on being told Dennis's sending-off for elbowing Tottenham's Ossie Ardiles (later a team-mate) was his 11th, **1987**.

THAT'S all people want to know. Is Mr Dennis playing?

DENNIS MONTAGUE, Yeovil director, on local interest in QPR's much-suspended left-back before FA Cup tie, **1988**.

Jimmy Dickinson

IF I can't outrun him, I'll hang up my boots.

BILLY BINGHAM, Luton winger, pointing to Portsmouth's 35-year-old Dickinson, who proceeded to outplay him, in Peter Jeffs, *Pompey's Gentleman Jim*, **1988**.

Peter Doherty

HE was almost a one-man team – and if Ireland had had two Dohertys that day, I shudder to think what might have happened. Peter almost played us off the park by himself. He scored four of the best goals you could wish to see and might have got another four but for Frank Swift. Even in defence Peter must have stopped us scoring twice as many as we did.

MAURICE EDELSTON on Ireland 4, Combined Services 7 in a wartime match at Windsor Park, in Bryon Butler and Ron Greenwood, *Soccer Choice*, **1979**.

Derek Dooley

I have never met a man who had such an eye for the quarter-chance – half-chances Derek regarded as sitters. . . . He was slow to get up speed, but once he did start moving he was like a whole herd of elephants on the rampage.

NEIL FRANKLIN, former England centre-half, in *Soccer at Home and Abroad*, **1956**. Dooley was a prolific scorer for Sheffield Wednesday before injury ended his career.

Duncan Edwards

THE Kohinoor diamond amongst our crown jewels. Even when he had won his first full England cap and was still eligible for our youth team, he used to love turning out at a lower level. He remained an unspoiled boy to the end, his head the same size it had been from the start. He just loved to play anywhere and with anyone.

JIMMY MURPHY, Manchester United assistant manager at the time of the Munich air crash.

John Fashanu

THE other half (with Dave Beasant) of the two-man team. Immensely strong, with genuine pace, he carries an enormous burden every time he goes on to the field and he discharges it with astonishing consistency.

JOHN GILES, ex-Leeds and Republic of Ireland player, **1988**.

NOT blessed with talented feet, but put the ball in front of him and he'll knock people out of the way to get it. Dangerous.

BRYAN ROBSON, England captain, **1988**.

Tom Finney

TOMMY Finney was grizzly strong. Tommy could run for a week. I'd have played him in his overcoat. There would have been four men marking him when we were kicking in. When I told people in Scotland that England were coming up with a winger who was better than Stanley Matthews, they laughed at me. But they weren't bloody laughing when Big Georgie Young was running all over Hampden Park looking for Tommy Finney.

BILL SHANKLY.

TOM told me that if I got tired I should play the ball out to him on the wing and he would keep hold of it until I got my breath back. He did it, too.

BOBBY ROBSON on Finney's advice to him on his England debut, **1988**.

I thought everybody would have forgotten the likes of me.

FINNEY on being honoured by Football Writers' Association, **1988**.

William ('Fatty') Foulke

A football wonder is Willie, the most talked-of player in the world. A Leviathan (22½ stone) with the agility of a bantam. The cheeriest of companions and in repartee as difficult to score against as when between the posts.

WILLIAM PICKFORD and ALFRED GIBSON in *Association Football and the Men who made it*, **1906**. Foulke played goalkeeper for England in 1897.

Trevor Francis

HE told me he had a system for taking penalties. I don't know what it is, but it's obviously bloody useless.

JIM SMITH, QPR manager, after Francis's second successive miss, **1988**.

Hughie Gallacher

WHEN I ran out onto the pitch there was suddenly a huge 'Ohhh' of disappointment. The crowd had just noticed how small I was. They thought I was far too wee.

HUGHIE GALLACHER, centre-forward for Scotland's 'Wembley Wizards', on his Newcastle United debut in **1926**.

Paul Gascoigne

HE had a round face, round body and round legs. But I've never seen such skill in a young player.

GEOFF WILSON, coach to Gascoigne's old school team, **1988**.

HE can be a loony with a fast mouth. He's either going to be one of the greats or finish up at 40 bitter about wasting such talent.

JOHN BAILEY, former Newcastle colleague, **1988**.

HE's a lovable young guy, the sort you'd take home to meet your mum and dad and he'd have them falling off the settee, rolling with laughter on the floor. It was significant to me that when Tottenham paid £2m to take him away, there wasn't one suggestion of 'good riddance' from the other players.

GLENN ROEDER, Newcastle captain, **1988**.

HE's like the golfer who's got all the shots. The question is – how good is he at selecting which shot and when?

HOWARD WILKINSON, Sheffield Wednesday manager, **1988**.

TOTTENHAM have signed a player with outstanding ability – and suspect temperament. Gazza's problem is that he is immature – on the field and off.

MIRANDHINA, Newcastle forward, **1988**.

THE immediate future cannot yet lie in the hands of players like Gascoigne. First he has to adjust to being with a big club like Tottenham. He has had two games so far. In one he was brought off and in the other he died. Not literally, but he did fade.

BOBBY ROBSON, England manager, **1988**.

STAY there fatty, I'll be back in a minute.

VINNY JONES, going to take a corner, to Gascoigne during their notorious confrontation, Wimbledon *v* Newcastle, **1988**.

PAUL Gascoigne has done more for Mars Bars than anyone since Marianne Faithfull.

PATRICK BARCLAY, the *Independent*, **1988**.

THEY can't call me the Mars Bar Boy anymore – it's more like the Cucumber Kid. I can't give up chocolate completely, but the barmy days of eating three Mars a day are behind me.

GASCOIGNE, **1988**.

GEORGE Best without brains.

STAN SEYMOUR, Newcastle chairman, **1988**.

HE is accused of being arrogant, unable to cope with the press, and a boozer. Sounds like he's got a chance to me.

GEORGE BEST, **1988**.

John Giles

THAT Johnny Giles of Leeds is a great player. Beats me why Alf Ramsey has never picked him for England.

WILLIE ORMOND, Scotland manager, **1973**.

AN incredible player. I thought he was miles better than Bremner. A better passer than Bremner; shrewder, more devious than Bremner; and harder when he wanted to be.

STEVE PERRYMAN, Spurs player, in *A Man For All Seasons*, **1985**.

I cannot even remember getting in a good tackle against him for he was quick and nippy and if there was the slightest chance of his being hurt you would suddenly be confronted by a full set of studs. He knew I was after him and once, after nipping me, Johnny gave me an impish grin and said: 'You will learn.' I did.

GRAEME SOUNESS in *No Half Measures*, **1985**.

Andy Gray

HIS style is more suited to Rugby Union.

UDO LATTEK, Bayern Munich coach, **1985**.

Eddie Gray

WHEN he plays on snow, he doesn't leave any footprints.

DON REVIE, Leeds manager, **1970**.

Jimmy Greaves

HE was always very calm, very collected and, where scoring goals was concerned, he was a Picasso.

CLIVE ALLEN, Spurs striker, in *There's Only One Clive Allen*, **1987**.

Bruce Grobbelaar

MUCH underrated because of his tendency to clown around – and make occasional mistakes. What is often overlooked is the level of his moral courage. He tackles problems around the box that so many goalkeepers, including the best of them, shy away from. A great asset.

JOHN GILES, **1989**.

Ruud Gullit

GREAVES: 'E's a Moroccan or something isn't 'e?
ST JOHN: Moluccan.
GREAVES: Yeah, Moluccan, that's it. Well blimey 'e can't half play a bit.

EXCHANGE on *Saint & Greavsie Show*, **1988**.

HE has everything, apart from a short-back-and-sides. He reminds me of a black John Charles. You can't plan for him. You can't mark him.

JOHN TOSHACK, Real Sociedad manager and ex-Wales striker, **1988**.

THE way to do it [stop Gullit] is to wind him up and stamp yourself on him. Before the game started I would try to be his best pal, talk to him about reggae . . . then when the whistle blew I'd turn into his worst enemy. It would make it all the harder for him to cope with.

VINNY JONES, Wimbledon midfielder, on how he would play the Dutch captain, **1988**.

HE can become the new Michel Platini of the 1988 European Championships. But a Maradona, that's another matter.

PLATINI, **1988**.

WHEN he gets mine back home he'll wonder who the bloody hell's it is.

MICK MCCARTHY, Republic of Ireland and former Barnsley defender, on swapping shirts with Gullit, **1988**.

IF all else fails, you could wait for the first corner and use his dreadlocks to tie him to a post.

VINNY JONES, **1988**.

Billy Hamilton (Northern Ireland)

IN another week special stars like Zico, Maradona and Hamilton will have gone home and Spain will be bankrupt.

BARCELONA NEWSPAPER, World Cup finals, **1982**.

Alan Hansen

A good skipper, but he could have been a really great one if he had been a bit more extrovert.

BOB PAISLEY, **1989**.

Ron Harris

WE'VE played Chelsea ten times, and he's been booked every time for tackles on me. George Best says in his book that all Harris can do is man-to-man mark, and that's right. If you thought, I'll stay with this geezer and wherever he runs, run with him, and just not be distracted . . . there's nothing I could do about it. Imagine what a trained athlete, a man like Harris, can do with his mind set – the ball could be there, two yards away, but all he wants to do is just stay here with me.

STAN BOWLES in **1976**. Harris was later a team-mate at Brentford.

I like to think that apart from being a bit of a butcher, I've something else to offer.

RON HARRIS, **1979**.

Glenn Hoddle

HODDLE a luxury? It's the bad players who are a luxury.

DANNY BLANCHFLOWER, **1981**.

BRAZIL don't expect Zico to tackle back. It might be worth taking a chance on a midfield player whose principal asset is not his lungs.

PETER SHREEVE, Tottenham coach, **1982**.

YOU can scare Hoddle out of a match and you couldn't depend on him to bring you a cup of tea if you were dying.

TOMMY SMITH, ex-Liverpool opponent, **1988**.

THE best passer of the ball in the world.

DON HOWE, England coach, before European Championships, in which Hoddle started on the subs' bench, **1988**.

I hear Glenn's found God. That must have been one hell of a pass.

JASPER CARROT, comedian, on Hoddle's emergence as a born-again Christian, **1988**.

Jim Holton

SIX foot two
Eyes of blue
Big Jim Holton's
After you.

MANCHESTER UNITED fans' chant, **1973**.

WE put bells on a football so he would know where it was. We had complaints from Morris Dancers saying he was kicking them all over the place.

TOMMY DOCHERTY, who bought him for United, **1988**.

WHEN I signed him from Shrewsbury for £100,000 Harry Gregg said, 'You've got a player who doesn't know the meaning of the word defeat.' A week later I phoned Harry back and said, 'Aye, and defeat's not the only word he doesn't know the meaning of. There's pass, control, dribble . . . .'

TOMMY DOCHERTY

A one-man grappling iron.

DAVID MEEK, *Manchester Evening News*, **1974**.

Mark Hughes

I bet every manager on the Continent would want him at the moment. He's not dirty, but you know you've been in a game when you've faced him. Mark's making the First Division pay for the tough time he had at Barcelona.

BRIAN HORTON, Oxford manager, **1989**.

Roger Hunt

YES, he misses a few. But he gets in the right places to miss them.

BILL SHANKLY, **1966**.

Norman Hunter

HE challenged for the ball as though his life depended on it. His attitude was quite daunting; it was as if he regarded being beaten as a personal affront, something to be remembered and later rectified. . . . There is no doubt that occasionally his tackling went beyond the boundaries of fair play.

TREVOR BROOKING in *100 Great British Footballers*, **1988**.

Geoff Hurst

DEEP down all the lads will be keeping a sort of score in their heads. Every time they jump for the ball and get it they'll be chalking it down. 'Three to me, one to Geoff Hurst' or whatever. Despite what the boss says he is special. Nicking the ball off a player like that, beating him in a tackle, is something you'll always remember. Magic!

PAUL PRICE, Tividale captain, before Tividale *v* Telford Cup tie, 1976–77. The Tividale manager had said that Hurst was just a Southern League player now. Brian James, *Journey to Wembley*, **1977**.

Leighton James

LEIGHTON came over to me just before kick-off and said he hoped I had a good game. I knew then I had him in my pocket. In the league I came from, the only time players spoke to each other was to trade uncomplimentary remarks.

DANNY MCGRAIN, Scotland full-back, in Hugh Keevins, *Celtic Greats*, **1988**.

YOU'RE very deceptive son – you're even slower than you look.

TOMMY DOCHERTY, then Derby manager.

Pat Jennings

HE might be a bit vulnerable to a hard low shot from the edge of the six-yard-box.

DON HOWE, Arsenal coach, **1983**.

SOMEWHERE in there the grace of a ballet dancer joins with the strength of an SAS squaddie, the dignity of an ancient king, the nerve of a bomb disposal officer.

EAMON DUNPHY, **1983**.

Jimmy Johnstone

ON my first day as Scotland manager I had to call off practice after half-an-hour because nobody could get the ball off wee Jimmy Johnstone.

TOMMY DOCHERTY, **1970**.

Vinny Jones

HE's incredibly loyal. Ask him to jump off the stand roof and he'd do it. But he's as thick as two short planks. He always grabbed the quiz-book on our coach trips so that he could ask the questions. That way he didn't have to answer.

ARNIE REED, physiotherapist at Wealdstone, Jones's first club, **1988**.

BELIEVE it or not, Vinny is a very disciplined lad. We asked him to do a job on Gazza [Newcastle's Paul Gascoigne] and he was first class.

DON HOWE, Wimbledon coach, after the infamous testicle-squeezing incident, **1988**.

I don't know what all the fuss is about. I wasn't even booked.

JONES, on Gascoigne incident, **1988**.

His tattoos are a bit frightening, but if I can get him to smile I'll be happy.

BRIAN HILL, referee, before FA Cup final, **1988**.

I hope his manager will discipline him, but I don't suppose it'll do any good. He's just so thick.

DEREK WOODHOUSE, amateur player and Isle of Wight postman elbowed in the face by Jones in a friendly, **1988**.

I have been a great ambassador for this club.

JONES on his disappointment at being overlooked for captaincy, **1988**.

GRAHAM Rix said everyone in the First Division knows I am a competitive player . . . blend that in with my little one-twos, my work at free-kicks, my diagonal passes, my 40-yard balls . . .

JONES, **1988**.

I want to be respected. I'd like to be like Trevor Brooking.

JONES, **1988**.

VINNY is a once-in-a-lifetime human being.

SAM HAMMAM, Wimbledon chairman on Jones's move to Leeds, **1989**.

In Don Revie's day he would not have got through the door let alone pulled on a Leeds shirt.

JOHN GILES, ex-Leeds midfielder, **1989**.

Kevin Keegan

KEVIN Keegan is so famous that when we were in the Casbah even the blind men were calling out his name.

LAWRIE MCMENEMY, **1983**.

KEVIN Keegan is the Julie Andrews of football.

DUNCAN MCKENZIE, **1981**.

To call Keegan a superstar is stretching a point. Skill-wise, there are a lot of better players around. He's not fit to lace my boots as a player.

GEORGE BEST after Keegan claimed Best had contributed to soccer's declining popularity, **1982**.

KEEGAN is not fit to lace Best's drinks.

JOHN ROBERTS, soccer writer, **1982**.

Denis Law

DENIS was in the class of di Stefano, because he could do everything, organize a side and score goals. His close control was not as good perhaps, but he beat people by his speed of thought.

HARRY GREGG, Manchester United team-mate, 1960s, in John Motson and John Rowlinson, *The European Cup 1955–80*, **1980**.

BUSBY knew how important he was. When Denis was doubtful the boss would practically be on his hands and knees hoping he could play.

HARRY GREGG, as above.

Gary Lineker

GARY has one area of his game he needs to improve if he wants to be acknowledged as a complete, all-round striker . . . he needs to work on his ability to dribble with the ball and to create his own chances, because there is no doubt he is a striker who relies on good and consistent service from team-mates. If that service isn't forthcoming his contribution to the game is limited.

TREVOR BROOKING, *100 Great British Footballers*, **1988**.

CONJUGATE the verb 'done great': I done great. He done great. We done great. They done great. The boy Lineker done great.

LETTER to the *Guardian*, after TV pundit Mick Channon, during World Cup, **1986**.

Nat Lofthouse

LOFTY the Lion of Vienna
Has retired from t'football field
It took a medical specialist
To make Lofthouse finally yield.

Like a centurion tank was our Nathan
Wi' a turn of speed like a bomb
Many a goalie's said sadly
'I wonder where that came from?'

Harry Gregg just after t'final
Went into Nat's for a beer
Who returned his money and told him
We don't charge goalkeepers here.

MR KAY of Tonge Moor, Lancashire, from 'Lofthouse Saga' on the Bolton and England centre-forward's retirement in **1960**.

Duncan McKenzie

HE is like a beautiful motor car. Six owners and been in the garage most of the time.

JOHN TOSHACK, Mersey derby opponent and broadcasting colleague, **1978**.

Steve McMahon

HE can be a little nasty when necessary – a bit of a rat in getting hold of the ball. But that's only because he wants his team to control the game. And once he has it he's a dream. Teams get 70 or 80 per cent of possession when he's in midfield – not five minutes of magic with the likes of Glenn Hoddle.

ALAN HUDSON, former England midfielder, **1988**.

HE arrived with a reputation as the tough guy we needed to replace Souness, but he got found out. He was all right when he was nipping people, but when they started nipping him back he didn't like it.

BOB PAISLEY, **1989**.

Paul McStay

ONLY a masochist could find a serious flaw in him, either as a player or as a human being. Sometimes I wonder if Paul might have made a better player if he had possessed a bigger ego, but I would never want to change him. I had a very healthy respect for people like Bobby Evans in the Fifties and then Paddy Crerand in the decade after that but, for awareness and skill, Paul is better than any of them, including Kenny Dalglish.

JOHN KELMAN, Celtic chief scout, in Hugh Keevins, *Celtic Greats*, **1988**.

ESSENTIALLY, Paul is still a Celtic supporter who also has a contract to play for the club.

KELMAN, as above.

Malcolm Macdonald

HE has criticized seven [Liverpool] players and he is not fit to lace just one boot of any of the seven. We played against him in the 1974 FA Cup final, and Phil Thompson reckons he still has him sitting on the mantelpiece waiting for him to show.

KENNY DALGLISH on Macdonald follow-up to Bob Paisley's criticisms of Liverpool, **1989**.

Wilf Mannion

HIS style is so graceful, and so courtly, that he wouldn't be out of place in a lace ruffle and the perruque.

DON DAVIES ('Old International'), the *Manchester Guardian*, **1950**.

Diego Maradona

MARADONA can win a game on his own in five minutes.

BOBBY ROBSON before **1986** World Cup quarter-finals. Maradona took him at his word.

PELE had nearly everything. Maradona *has* everything. He works harder, does more and is more skilful. Trouble is that he'll be remembered for another reason. He bends the rules to suit himself.

SIR ALF RAMSEY after Maradona's 'handball' goal *v* England, **1986**.

THE best one-footed player since Puskas.

SIR STANLEY MATTHEWS in Mexico City, **1986**.

WITH Maradona, even Arsenal would have won the World Cup.

BOBBY ROBSON, **1986**.

I was dancing in a discotheque when all of a sudden this very small, fat man approached and started hugging me. I thought it was a fan and then his bodyguard came over. Then I recognized him.

RUUD GULLIT, Holland captain, on meeting Maradona, **1988**.

Rodney Marsh

I believed that Rodney's touch of theatre, his marvellous skill, could be the element which finally snapped United's hold in the city. I suspect that if you asked Manchester City fans today whether I did the right thing in signing Marsh they would answer a firm yes. They have learned to live with his extravagances, his inconsistencies. It is, after all, the inevitable price you pay for the promise of magic.

MALCOLM ALLISON in *Colours of My Life*, **1975**.

Stanley Matthews

HE was the opposite of glamorous: a non-drinker, a non-smoker, careful with his money, brought up among thrift and the ever-looming threat of dole and debt. . . . He came from that England which had no reason to know that the Twenties were naughty and the Thirties had style.

ARTHUR HOPCRAFT, in *The Football Man*, **1968**.

STAN was unique. He never went for 50–50 balls, didn't score many goals, and was not good in the air. But on his day he was unplayable. He beat fellows so easily, with such pace and balance, often taking on four or five at a time.

JOE MERCER in David Meek, *Anatomy of a Football Star: George Best*, **1970**.

YOU usually knew how he would beat you. You could not do anything about it though.

DANNY BLANCHFLOWER in David Meek, *Anatomy of a Football Star: George Best*, **1970**.

THA can tell tha father from me that if he fancies chasing Brother Matthews here around for ninety minutes, then I'll swap jobs with tha father anytime and I'll have his wages and he can have mine.

TOMMY BANKS, Bolton and England player of the **1950s**, countering arguments at Professional Footballers' Association (PFA) meeting that, compared to factory workers, footballers were already well paid.

HE is an extraordinarily difficult winger to play alongside. It is sometimes impossible to anticipate what he is going to do next, and that means we are no longer a single team unit – which is what I understand as football.

RAICH CARTER, **1950**.

HE cut his partners out of the game. If you passed to him, you'd never see the ball again.

RAY BOWDEN, Matthews's first international partner in 1934, in Michael George, *Sportsmen of Cornwall*, **1986**.

> LAST night I had the strangest dream
> I've never had before
> Stan Matthews on the wing for Stoke
> At the age of 84

SONG on Keele University students' Rag Record, **1964**.

STAN Matthews used to put the ball on my centre-parting. They don't do that any more.

TOMMY LAWTON, former England centre-forward, **1985**.

I'M not a scientist; I'm not a poet; I'm not a writer. But of course I am very honoured.

SIR STAN on receiving honorary degree from Keele, **1987**.

Joe Mercer

THEY wouldn't last a postman his morning round.

DIXIE DEAN, **1930s** Everton colleague, on Mercer's spindly, bandy legs.

Jackie Milburn

THE roar of the crowd told me he was exceptional. I could sense his pace, the dramatic presence. I didn't need eyes.

GERRY BRERETON, blind entertainer, on Milburn's death, **1988**.

Joe Miller

WHEN you see him in his clothes he's like a wee boy with his suit too big. When he changes into a football strip he's graceful. He has magnetism. As soon as he gets the ball the backsides come off the seats. Best had it, Law had it. This wee lad's got it again.

BILLY MCNEILL, Celtic manager on his signing from Aberdeen, **1988**.

Mirandinha

TRAINER: How are you feeling?
MIRANDINHA: I'm very well, thank you, how are you?

EXCHANGE as the Brazilian lay injured in a match soon after his arrival at Newcastle, **1987**.

HE's always in demand for things like opening shops, which must have helped him settle in quickly.

CHRIS WADDLE, ex-Newcastle, on Mirandinha's reception on Tyneside, **1988**.

ONE of their defenders said he would break my leg when he came to Newcastle. I think I will have a hamstring injury when that match is played.

MIRANDINHA, on playing at Portsmouth, **1988**.

SOME of the things I've seen him do on the training ground have been out of this world, others have been out of the kindergarten.

JIM SMITH, Newcastle manager, **1988**.

Bobby Moore

BOBBY was great at that. Someone would come and kick a lump out of him, and he'd play as though he hadn't even noticed. But ten minutes later . . . whoof! . . . He had a great 'golden boy' image, Mooro. But he was *hard*.

GEOFF HURST, West Ham and England team-mate, 1960s–1970s, in Brian James, *Journey to Wembley*, **1977**.

Pat Nevin

THE first post-punk footballer.

NEW MUSICAL EXPRESS, **1985**.

THE first yuppie of football.

CHELSEA INDEPENDENT fanzine, **1988**.

Charlie Nicholas

IF you don't get in the box and gamble, you are never going to score goals. It's a question of getting in there, and getting in before defenders, not waiting. Then you get the ones that hit you and go in off your knee, or your face. But Charlie wants to jink past someone, then bend it in from eighteen yards where the keeper can see it coming.

TONY WOODCOCK on his partnership with Nicholas at Arsenal, *Inside Soccer*, **1985**.

I'D like someone to tell me the reasons Nicholas was put in quarantine at Highbury. Somebody must be barmy. It was like buying a Van Gogh painting then sticking it away in a bank vault.

BRIAN CLOUGH on Arsenal's leaving Nicholas in the reserves, **1987**.

CHARLIE has to look hard at the situation and ask himself why he has failed to fulfil his potential in England. It is all right blaming the club, the coaching staff or the manager, but it has happened too many times.

GEORGE GRAHAM, Arsenal manager, on selling Nicholas, **1988**.

HE only has two arms and legs, same as the rest of our players, but once he finds his feet I'm convinced he'll do well.

IAN PORTERFIELD, Aberdeen manager, on buying him, **1988**.

STRINGFELLOW'S will miss him.

JIMMY GREAVES, **1988**.

WE talked about football but really all he wanted to talk about was sex. . . . I hear he's not been scoring many goals recently and that's why he left Arsenal, but all I can tell you is he certainly scored a hat-trick with me that night.

THEREZA BAZAR, pop singer with Dollar, **1988**.

I know I had the reputation of a playboy in London, but I don't want to say much about it, because a lot of it was paper talk.

NICHOLAS on returning to Scotland, **1988**.

HE needs one touch too many to be a world-class player.

JOHN GILES, **1988**.

Steve Nicol

THE most complete player in British football, the best two-footed player in the game, (but) not exactly a deep thinker.

MARK LAWRENSON, ex-Liverpool team-mate, **1988**.

HE's a walking advert for the benefits of junk food. He'll eat five packets of crisps and wash it down with Coke and Mars bars.

LAWRENSON, as above.

Pele

PELE does everything superbly with the possible exception of taking a dive in an opponent's penalty area. He has to learn about that art, though with his skills I can't think why he bothers to lower himself and start acting.

MARTIN PETERS in *Mexico 70*, **1970**

Martin Peters

MARTIN Peters is a player ten years ahead of his time.

ALF RAMSEY, **1968**.

MARTIN Peters? He's the one who's ten years ahead of his time, so we've got to wait for him to come good.

MALCOLM ALLISON, **1970**.

Michel Platini

EVEN his feet are intelligent.

MICHEL HIDALGO, France manager, **1984**.

I couldn't believe the way Platini spoke to his team-mates. He was always yapping and yelling.

RANDY SAMUEL, Canada's centre-half, after defeat by France, World Cup, **1986**.

Ferenc Puskas

HIS shooting was unbelievable and his left foot was like a hand, he could do anything with it. In the showers he would even juggle with the soap.

FRANCISCO GENTO, Real Madrid team-mate 1950–60s, in Motson and Rowlinson, *The European Cup 1955–80*, **1980**.

Alf Ramsey

RAMSEY – tha's as much use as a chocolate teapot.

MICHAEL PARKINSON, quoting fan's comment as winger Johnny Kelly skinned Alf Ramsey – Barnsley *v* Southampton, **1950s**.

ALF was never a great one for small talk when he was with England parties; football was his one subject of conversation. He was always a pepper-and-salt man, working out moves and formations with the cruets on the table.

JACKIE MILBURN, an England team-mate, in Max Marquis, *Anatomy of a Football Manager*, **1970**.

Kevin Ratcliffe

OVER short distances Kevin is unbeatable, the Carl Lewis of Goodison. He's as hard as nails as well. Some of his tackling is too much at times and he gets away with murder, he's got such an innocent looking face.

ANDY GRAY, ex-Everton team-mate, in *Shades of Gray*, **1986**.

Peter Reid

EVERTON'S most important signing since the war.

HOWARD KENDALL, manager, in *Everton Scrapbook*, **1986**.

HE used to make us all laugh at Everton on a Monday morning. Peter, you see, enjoyed himself on a weekend when the game was over and liked a swift pint or two at Benny's in Manchester, and when he turned up for training on Monday Reidy always looked a little jaded. During the week he was perhaps the laziest player in the squad, and was quite often excused training. (But) we all knew that come a match Reidy would be out there covering every blade of grass.

ANDY GRAY in *Shades of Gray*, **1986**.

I'M not a Glenn Hoddle, hitting 40-yard passes straight to a striker. But I can win it, keep it and knock little killer balls.

REID, **1988**.

I try not to dwell too much on the age bit. I feel as sharp now over the first five or six yards as ever I did – we'll not talk about what happens after that.

REID, **1988**.

Graham Roberts

GRAHAM has kicked a few in England, now he can go and kick some in Scotland.

DAVID PLEAT, Tottenham manager, on selling Roberts to Rangers, **1987**.

Bryan Robson

I wish I was England coach because I'd teach Bryan Robson not to kick and foul people when things go wrong.

BRIAN CLOUGH, **1983**.

ENGLAND's Captain Marvel.

BOBBY ROBSON, England manager, **1989**.

Ian Rush

PAINFUL to watch, but beautiful.

DAVID PLEAT after Rush had scored five against his Luton side, **1983**.

A very intelligent player. Not in the sense of doing crosswords or answering quizzes on the coach to away trips, but as a player he is very sharp. You never start level with Rushie.

KEVIN RATCLIFFE, Wales colleague and Everton captain, **1987**.

HE's a ghost. He's there but nobody can see him.

JUVENTUS team-mate during Rush's barren run, **1988**.

IT's like Bradman coming out to bat with 500 on the board already.

CHARLTON fan watching Rush appear as substitute in his first match after returning from Turin, **1988**.

Bill Shankly

SHANKS is getting past it. He's letting the left-half take his own throw-ins.

EVERTON player to Joe Mercer.

Kevin Sheedy

HE'S so good, he plays as though he were a Brazilian.

HOWARD KENDALL, Athletic Bilbao and former Everton manager, **1988**.

Peter Shilton

I'VE seen forwards get past me with all the confidence of a Pele or a Johan Cruyff and then, faced by 'Shilts', suddenly lose their nerve. I mean, it's happened to me when I've tried to beat him in training. All he has to do is crouch a little bit, and he sort of spreads and fills the bloody goal up.

LARRY LLOYD, in Jason Tomas, *The Magnificent Obsession*, **1982**.

Tommy Smith

THE king of 'em all . . . the best pro I've ever met. He must have played about two million six-a-sides in his day. But this morning he'd have fought his best mate over a throw-in.

EMLYN HUGHES, Liverpool team-mate, 1960s–70s, in Brian James, *Journey to Wembley*, **1977**.

Graeme Souness

TOMMY Smith with a Rolls Royce engine.

JOHN ROBERTS, *Daily Mail*, **1984**.

THERE is black and white proof I'm not the killer I'm supposed to be. I've only been sent off twice.

SOUNESS, in *No Half Measures*, **1985**.

THE only things I have retained from my wilder days are a taste for vintage champagne and the nickname Charlie.

SOUNESS, as above.

WHEN I was at Spurs I was always a Middlesbrough fan who'd always supported Liverpool, and the only team I would have moved to Italy for would have been Sampdoria because, when I was a boy I used to skip school in Edinburgh and sneak into Italy to watch them. But as I stood there cheering on Sampdoria I couldn't forget that as a foetus I was an avid Rangers fan.

'GRAEME SOUNESS' as portrayed on *Only An Excuse*, BBC Radio Scotland spoof documentary, **1986**.

THEY serve a drink in Glasgow called the Souness – one half and you're off.

TOMMY DOCHERTY, **1988**.

IF he was a chocolate drop, he'd eat himself.

ARCHIE GEMMILL, Scotland team-mate, **1978**.

Neville Southall

WE were beginning to think he was only human.

COLIN HARVEY, Everton manager, on his goalkeeper's 'miraculous' saves at West Ham, **1988**.

Alfredo di Stefano

HE was one of the greatest, if not the greatest footballer I had ever seen. At that time we had forwards and defenders doing separate jobs, but he did everything.

MATT BUSBY in Motson and Rowlinson, *The European Cup 1955–80*, **1980**.

MOST of all, he would make us want to win. Whenever we practised, even when we played cards or basketball in the gym, he would want to win. When I became a manager I realized how important it was to have a player like that on the field.

FRANCISCO GENTO, Real Madrid team-mate in six European Cup finals, 1956–62, in *The European Cup 1955–80*.

Paul Stewart

NONE of our players is for sale and that is definite. Stewart has just signed a four-year contract so he is not going anywhere. So far as Tottenham Hotspur are concerned, there has been no contact.

PETER SWALES, Manchester City chairman, February 1988.

MY heart is in this club [City].

STEWART, March 1988.

THIS has got to be the most fantastic weekend of my life. Tomorrow I get married to my girlfriend, Beverley, and on Sunday I sign for Spurs.

STEWART, June 1988.

Nobby Stiles

AN assassin. Brutal, badly intentioned and a bad sportsman.

OTTO GLORIA, Benfica manager, in The European Cup 1955–80.

I stood in front of [Paul] Gascoigne to cut off any service. I got the idea from watching a video of Nobby Stiles marking Eusebio.

VINNY JONES, Wimbledon player, 1988.

THE players' player, bête noire of the purists, a tiny, toothless, urban, gesticulating figure, perennially in the bad books of referees and opponents . . . a player with no obvious physical or technical gifts, a poor passer of the ball, but a formidable marker and an extraordinary competitor.

BRIAN GLANVILLE, in The History of the World Cup, 1980.

Gordon Strachan

HE was playing much of the time from memory. But by God, what a memory.

RON ATKINSON, Manchester United manager, on Strachan's comeback after injury, **1985**.

Bert Trautmann

WHAT manner of man is Trautmann? Certainly not one you would pass in a crowd. He is of the Nordic type, with blond hair, keen grey eyes, a gentle manner, a charming smile, and a deceptive air of indolence in repose. But a steely look can come in those grey eyes; the thrust of a panther's spring into those clean, straight limbs; and few can pass with such lightning rapidity from complete immobility to energetic action. In straightforwardness and clean living he is a model for any young boy.

H. D. DAVIES on Manchester City's German goalkeeper in *Boy's Own Paper*, **1957**.

Marco van Basten

HE doesn't even influence the play very much, but he decides matches.

JOHAN CRUYFF, former Holland captain, **1988**.

HE has a special ability to see goals and make space where there appears to be none.

RUUD GULLIT, Holland and Milan team-mate, **1988**.

Pat van den Hauwe

AN impressive pro, I particularly like his willingness to get on the ball and play.

JOHN GILES on the Everton enforcer, **1989**.

Terry Venables

A clever, cocky player – arrogant, but then he was good.

MIKE PEJIC, ex-Stoke, Everton and England defender, **1988**.

Bertie Vogts (West Germany)

A team of eleven Bertie Vogtses would be unbeatable.

KEVIN KEEGAN, **1975**.

Norman Whiteside

HE came at me like the Karate Kid.

DAVID O'LEARY, Arsenal defender, **1987**.

I don't really like playing against the clever ones like Gascoigne. I prefer someone like Whiteside, where you can get stuck in, get a bit back, and have a good laugh about it.

VINNY JONES, **1988**.

Ray Wilkins

HE can't run, can't tackle and can't head a ball. The only time he goes forward is to toss the coin.

TOMMY DOCHERTY, **1987**. Wilkins was nicknamed 'The Crab' by Ron Atkinson.

HE played the game in the Liverpool fashion and I could never understand why he was criticized for that.

TREVOR BROOKING, *100 Great British Footballers*, **1988**.

Ray Wilson

I don't think that I ever gave many fouls away. The most was when I played [for Huddersfield] against Stanley Matthews in his comeback game for Stoke City. I coughed twice and the referee blew.

RAY WILSON, former England full-back, in Martin Tyler, *Boys of '66*, **1981**.

Tony Woodcock

HE's fast, strong, sharp and skilful but otherwise he's useless.

KEN BROWN, Norwich manager, **1982**.

Frank Worthington

THE way he's losing his hair he'll be the first bald guy ever to do impressions of Elvis Presley.

GRAEME SOUNESS, **1984**.

Ron Yeats

HE's a colossus. Come outside and I'll give you a walk round him.

BILL SHANKLY on his 6ft 2in, 14st signing from Dundee United, **1961**.

WITH him at centre half, we could play Arthur Askey in goal.

SHANKLY, **1962**.

Clubs and Teams

Arsenal 1920s–30s

ONLY people who will not spend big money on transfer fees need apply.

ARSENAL advertisement in *Athletic News* for post of secretary-manager, **1925**. Herbert Chapman got the job.

ALTHOUGH I do not suggest that the Arsenal go on the defensive *even* for tactical purposes, I think it may be said that some of their best scoring chances have come when they have been driven back and then have broken away to strike suddenly and swiftly.

HERBERT CHAPMAN, Arsenal manager, **1930s**.

AT Highbury we went for results. Results meant getting goals so we cut the movements down from four passes to two. Our great ball was the long one and that opened the game up.

TED DRAKE, Arsenal and England centre-forward in *The Encyclopedia of Association Football*, **1960**.

I well remember that as a boy, there was only one club for me – Arsenal.

PUSKAS in *Captain of Hungary*, **1955**.

YOU'LL have to watch these Trojans. They don't play your game: they play an attacking game.

GEORGE ALLISON, Arsenal manager, acting himself doing pre-match talk in film, *The Arsenal Stadium Mystery*, **1939**.

Arsenal Post-War

THE place was like a palace. You were immediately conscious of belonging to something really big, really important. Everyone at Highbury lived, breathed, talked, ate and drank Arsenal. Everyone believed in the club; everyone was proud to be part of it. It was just like playing cricket for Yorkshire.

BRIAN CLOSE, England cricketer, on his spell with Arsenal (1950–51) in *I Don't Bruise Easily*, **1978**.

PEOPLE still expect more of Arsenal than they do of most other teams. If one of our players commits a foul the other team's supporters are appalled.

DENIS HILL-WOOD. Old Etonian and Arsenal chairman, in Arthur Hopcraft, *The Football Man*, **1968**.

IT seems ridiculous when I look at all that silverware, but also very wonderful. I believe that the present team is the greatest that has ever represented Arsenal.

DENIS HILL-WOOD, chairman, on **1971** 'double' team.

IF he [Osvaldo Ardiles] had gone to Arsenal, they would have had him marking the opposing goalkeeper or something.

DANNY BLANCHFLOWER, **1981**.

WHEN Wimbledon hit long balls up to a 6′ 2″ black centre forward, it's destroying the game. When Arsenal hit long balls to a 6′ 4″ Irishman, it's good football.

DAVE BASSETT, then Wimbledon manager, **1986**. The players were John Fashanu and Niall Quinn.

Arsenal 1986–89

THE Anfield axiom is the classic one . . . treat the ball like a diamond, win it, hold it, polish it, and use it. The emphasis of this otherwise excellent Arsenal team is different. Too often they play the ball back to goalkeeper John Lukic.

JOHN GILES, ex-Leeds and Republic of Ireland player, **1988**.

ARSENAL? Spurs? No chance. The two best clubs in London are still Stringfellow's and The Hippodrome.

TERRY MCDERMOTT, ex-Liverpool midfielder, dismissing London's challenge to Anfield in October, **1988**. Arsenal went on to win the title . . . at Liverpool.

THEY play in a certain way which is not my way. We have to give them a bit of credit, but we have to look at ourselves for the reasons we lost.

KENNY DALGLISH, Liverpool manager, after Arsenal's last-gasp title win, **1989**.

Blackburn Rovers 1880s

ALL hail, ye gallant Rover lads!
Etonians thought you were but cads:
They've found a football game their dads
By meeting Blackburn Rovers.

SONG before the **1882** FA Cup final. The Old Etonians won 1–0.

Bolton Wanderers 1950s

WHEN I first came into the game, Bolton were the team everybody feared for their sheer brute force. Their England international full-back Tommy Banks used to say to Chelsea winger Peter Brabrook: 'If thou tries to get past me, lad, thou will get gravel rash. . . .' And a favourite comment from their rugged half-back Doug Hennin was: 'If my inside-forward 'appens to come through, chip him back to me . . .'

JIMMY GREAVES in *This One's On Me*, **1979**.

Brazil 1970

THE Romanians were hard, but as far as I was concerned the Brazilians were harder; and if that seemed difficult to believe, I had the bruises and the soreness to prove my point. Jairzinho went right over the top of the ball and kicked my shins. . . . Pele had a go at me and I landed one back, so that was twice I had lost my temper which is unusual for me.

MARTIN PETERS at the Mexico World Cup, **1970**.

Brechin City

IN their long and illustrious history, 1906–86 – or, as they're known here, the wilderness years – records have come easily to Brechin City. They were the first club to dabble in sponsorship, when the people of Brechin offered them money to go to play somewhere else.

ONLY AN EXCUSE, BBC Radio Scotland spoof documentary, **1986**.

Celtic 1967

HIS [Robert Kelly, the chairman] was the brain that fashioned the organization with Stein at its head. If he had a weakness it was his obsession with the players of the past and especially the great Celtic team of before the First World War. The accolade was put on the trip [to Lisbon] when he declared solemnly and it seemed with some pain: 'This was the greatest Celtic team of all time.' He might have expanded the adjective to Scottish or even British and nobody would have questioned his judgement.

JOHN RAFFERTY, *Scotsman* soccer correspondent, in *We'll Support You Evermore*, **1976**.

WE don't just want to win this cup. We want to do it playing good football, to make neutrals glad we've won it, glad to remember how we did it.

JOCK STEIN Celtic manager, before 2–1 European Cup final win by his 'Lisbon Lions' over Inter Milan, **1967**.

Charlton Athletic 1930s

UNMATCHED by the record of any club in the British Isles, cradle of Association Football, or Soccer, the history of Charlton Athletic, one of the most sensational aggregations of the booting game ever to essay an invasion of the United States and Canada, is truly monumental in athletic annals.

PROGRAMME NOTES, Illinois All Stars *v* Charlton in Chicago, **1937**.

Chelsea

CHELSEA are the most unusual of clubs. They have never done what every other club was doing at the same time as every other club was doing it.

RALPH FINN in *A History of Chelsea FC*, **1969**.

IT's true to say that at Chelsea Football Club the manager has never been judged on his results, because the manager's results have been very bad.

GRAHAM SMITH, Chelsea director, announcing that John Hollins's coach Ernie Walley had been replaced by Bobby Campbell, **1988**.

IF Chelsea can't make ends meet through soccer, they should, like any commercial concern, go out of business, or move to another ground.

EMILE AL-UZAIZI, Hammersmith and Fulham Conservative councillor, opposing Chelsea's plan for redeveloping Stamford Bridge to fight off owners Marler Estates, **1988**.

COMMODORE already sponsors Tessa Sanderson, Chelsea FC and a football team, Bayern Munich.

COMPUTER GUARDIAN, **1988**.

The Corinthians

THE Corinthians of my day never trained, and I can safely say that the need of it was never felt. We were all fit and I think I could have played on for more than one and a half hours without being any the worse.

G. O. SMITH, centre-forward 1893–1901, in Edward Grayson, *Corinthians, Casuals and Cricketers*, **1955**.

England 1950

THEY congratulated us, though I knew how they must have felt. They showed the stiff upper lip which Hitler could never understand.

CHUBBY LYONS, USA manager, after 1–0 victory over England in World Cup, **1950**.

To be defeated by the United States at football was like the MCC being beaten by Germany at cricket.

BILLY WRIGHT, England skipper, in *Captain of England*, **1950**.

England 1966

PEOPLE say England are a physical team. They have left out a word. They should say England are a physically fit team.

HAROLD SHEPHERDSON, trainer, on World Cup-winning team.

YOU'VE beaten them once. Now go out and bloody beat them again.

ALF RAMSEY to England team before extra time in the final victory over West Germany.

As we came round the corner from the eighteenth green a crowd of members were at the clubhouse window cheering and waiting to tell me that England had won the World Cup. It was the blackest day of my life.

DENIS LAW, Scottish international and patriot, in *An Autobiography*, **1979**.

ENGLAND'S victory could be a decisive factor in strengthening sterling . . . It was a tremendous, gallant fight that England won. Our men showed real guts and the bankers, I suspect, will be influenced by this, and the position of the Government correspondingly strengthened.

RICHARD CROSSMAN MP, Labour minister, in *Diaries of a Cabinet Minister, 1964–70*.

AND does it mean anything except that we've got a good football team and an even better manager in Alf Ramsey? Probably not, although I'd like to draw the moral (not for the first time) that there's nothing wrong with Britain; it's just our politicians that let us down.

NIGEL LAWSON, later Chancellor of the Exchequer, in *The Spectator*, **1966**.

THEY canna play nane.

JIM BAXTER before England *v* Scotland, **1967**. Scotland won 3–2.

England 1970

THE English team had some outstanding players. Men like Banks, and Bobby Moore, and Cooper and Bobby and Jack Charlton. They can play on any Brazilian team at any time – and that is no light compliment.

PELE after Brazil's victory over England, in *My Life and the Beautiful Game*, **1977**.

England 1988

I have a sneaking suspicion that all the other countries involved will be much more wary of England than we will be of them.

BOBBY ROBSON, manager, at the start of the European Championship year.

OUR most priceless asset is our ability to score goals from anywhere.

ROBSON before the Championship. England scored only four more goals in six matches before the end of the year.

THEY may be joint favourites in England, but I'm not sure they are joint favourites in Europe – unless Ladbrokes have opened up over there.

JACK CHARLTON, Republic of Ireland manager, dismissing English optimism before the finals.

ENGLAND have some great players, but they are only great in England.

LEO BEENHAKKER, Real Madrid's Dutch coach, before European debacle, **1988**.

MAYBE we're not as good as we thought we were.

BOBBY ROBSON after the tournament had brought three defeats in three games.

WE didn't play very well, but it's not as if we committed a crime or anything.

GARY LINEKER.

ENGLAND play the game like old-fashioned gentlemen. Why are you so far behind the rest? You are 20 years behind. You are strong, but do things all wrong.

IGOR BELANOV, Soviet Union captain, after England's 3–1 defeat.

Estudiantes (1968 World Club champions)

WE tried to find out everything possible about our rivals individually, their habits, their characters, their weaknesses and even about their private lives, so that we could goad them on the field, get them to react and risk being sent off.

JUAN RAMON VERNON, Estudiantes player of 1968, talking in **1983**.

Everton

PRINCESS MARGARET: But Mr Labone, where *is* Everton?
BRIAN LABONE: In Liverpool, Ma'am.
PRINCESS MARGARET: Of course, we had your first team here last year.

BILL SHANKLY story of **1966** FA Cup final.

THIS team will dominate the seventies . . . nothing will stop it
becoming one of the greatest club teams of all times.

MERSEYSIDE SOCCER CORRESPONDENT in **1970**. The decade was dominated by
Liverpool.

FACING them on Saturday is like going into hospital for an
operation; you would rather not do it but the doctor says you must.

HOWARD WILKINSON, Sheffield Wednesday manager, preparing for FA Cup tie
against his club's bogey team. After two draws, Everton won 5–0, **1988**.

Holland 1988

WE dominated European club competitions when we were
involved, while Dutch football is at its lowest ebb for years.

ARTHUR COX, Derby Manager, **1988**. Within 10 weeks PSV Eindhoven had won the
European Cup and Holland the European Championships.

DURING the European Championships we went out every night until
two or three in the morning. The problem with Italians is that they
don't like to go out after playing.

RUUD GULLIT, Dutch captain, **1988**.

DON'T talk to me about Dutch creation – it was the sort of goal you
see in the Third Division every Saturday.

BOBBY ROBSON on third Dutch goal *v* England, European Championships **1988**.

Hungary 1953-54

THE Hungarians were just as great a team of pure
footballers in the years 1936–39 as they were when they beat us at
Wembley. But there was one vital difference . . . to the post- war
Hungarian, to be a great footballer was a passport to a good living
in a country where life wasn't very pleasant. Therefore their

football became much more pungent, much more incisive, much more determined, much more ultimate in its performance. Where it was a performance of art and craft before, it was a performance again, but now with a goal – and I mean goal in both senses. Their finishing was meant. If they didn't finish, they famished.

ARTHUR ROWE in *The Encyclopedia of Association Football*, **1960**.

THE legend grew that Hungary played football on the carpet and used mainly short passes. . . . The actual figure of long passes was as many as ninety-four, most of them played in the first hour of the match. More than sixty were in the air. The general impression, too, was that Hungary's six goals were scored by means of clever movements which contained many short passes. Here again, the facts showed a different picture to the one which existed in the mind of the Press and the public. Only *one* of Hungary's goals came from a move which started in their half of the field.

STAN CULLIS, Wolves manager 1950s, in *All for the Wolves*, **1960**.

THE 1954 Hungarian soccer masters did not go into the record books as the champions of the world. But they went into my personal memory file – and that of millions of other football-lovers – as the finest team ever to sort out successfully the intricacies of this wonderful game.

TOM FINNEY, Preston and England forward, in *Finney on Football*, **1958**.

Leeds United 1965–75

You Get Nowt for Coming Second.

BILLY BREMNER book title, **1969**. Leeds finished League runners-up five times.

THROUGHOUT the game they yapped at us. The man who was marking me asked if I'd won my Irish caps working for Wimpey. That didn't bother me half as much as the fact that [Gary] Sprake was throwing in goals.

JOHN GILES on Leeds's 1971 FA Cup defeat by Fourth Division Colchester, **1989**.

LEEDS should have been instantly relegated after being branded one of the dirtiest clubs in Britain. I feel strongly that the two pence-ha'penny suspended fine is the most misguided piece of woolly thinking ever perpetrated by the FA, a body hardly noted for its commonsense. It's like breathalysing a drunken driver, getting a positive reading, giving him his keys back and telling him to watch it on the way home.

BRIAN CLOUGH, August **1973** – a year before he became Leeds manager.

WE had seven, eight, nine years of Leeds, and that was too much. They played foul football, and showed that you could get away with cheating. So players come in with kicks and bruises all over them, and get their pay packets and think, 'No win bonus again; perhaps it's time we started this lark.'

ARTHUR ROWE in *Foul! Book of Football*, **1975**.

LOOKING back over the outstanding club sides in England over the past thirty years, I suppose Leeds have to be ranked alongside the Manchester United side that was partially destroyed at Munich, the United side of the late Sixties which boasted Best, Law and Charlton, the Liverpool side of the Seventies, the Arsenal double-winning side, and the Spurs side of the early Sixties.

BOBBY ROBSON, in *Time on the Grass*, **1982**.

ALLAN asked me for two things before the match, a car-park ticket and the winning goal. I obliged with both.

WAYNE CLARKE, brother of ex-Leeds striker Allan and scorer of Everton's goal which prevented Liverpool beating Leeds's record unbeaten start, **1988**.

LIVERPOOL (1987–88) are a good side with some great individuals who, like the old Dutch international team, don't play to a set formation and are far more flamboyant than Leeds were. We were a regiment. Everyone knew his job and stuck to it. We would have restricted Liverpool's space. We had ball-winners who could mark people out, something that few First Division players can do today. We would have frustrated Liverpool – and got more of the ball as the game wore on.

TERRY YORATH, Swansea manager, and Leeds player under Don Revie, **1988**.

It is often said no club has a divine right to be in the First Division
. . . well we bloody have.

THE HANGING SHEEP, Leeds fanzine, **1988**. Leeds had been in the Second since
1982.

Liverpool 1962–86

I want to build a team that's invincible, so they'll have to send a
team from Mars to beat us.

BILL SHANKLY, manager, **1971**.

It was one of Bill Shankly's ideas. A bit of psychology. Playing here
lifts good pros, puts the bad 'uns under pressure. We counted . . .
there were more bad pros about than good 'uns. So the sign went
up.

BOB PAISLEY, Shankly's successor, explaining the 'This is Anfield' plaque over the
players tunnel. Brian James, *Journey to Wembley*, **1977**.

LIVERPOOL are the most uncomplicated side in the world. They all
drive forward when they've got the ball, and they all get behind it
when they haven't.

JOE MERCER, **1973**.

THE team of our time, the ideal model of the contemporary team in
which collective qualities have risen above individual qualities, as
outstanding as such famous clubs as Real Madrid and Ajax.

MILIAN MILJANIC, Yugoslavia manager.

WE do things together. I'd walk into the toughest dockside pub in
the world with this lot. Because you know that if things got tough,
nobody would 'bottle' it, and scoot off.

EMLYN HUGHES on his Liverpool colleagues in 1976–77, in Brian James, *Journey to
Wembley*, **1977**.

MIND, I've been here during the bad times too. One year we came
second.

BOB PAISLEY, **1979**.

A lot of teams beat us, do a lap of honour and don't stop running. They live too long on one good result. I remember Jimmy Adamson crowing after Burnley had beaten us once that his players were in a different league. At the end of the season they were.

BOB PAISLEY, **1979**.

FOR those of you watching in black and white, Liverpool are the team with the ball.

JOKE by Liverpool fans before 1984 Milk Cup final *v* Everton, from Brian Barwick and Gerald Sinstadt, *The Great Derbies, Everton v Liverpool*, **1988**.

IT was not the Liverpool we are used to seeing. I don't know what they were trying to do, and I don't think they knew either.

KEVIN RATCLIFFE, Everton captain in February **1986**. Three months later Liverpool had done the double.

Liverpool 1987–89

BEFORE it was balls into channels for Rush. Now it's balls into channels, balls to feet, balls every-bloody-where.

JOHN SILLETT, Coventry manager, **1987**.

As we all knew would happen as soon as Rush went abroad, Liverpool have fallen to pieces.

TED CROKER, FA secretary, as Liverpool advanced to League title, **1988**.

THE only way to beat them is to let the ball down.

ALAN BALL, Portsmouth manager, **1988**.

IT was a case of barbed wire, building a dam and hoping for the best. They come towards you like a tidal wave.

STEVE THOMPSON, Charlton defender, **1988**.

(LIVERPOOL) are rigid but fluid, better than anyone at organizing themselves to defend for when the attack is finished.

DAVE SEXTON, England Under-21 manager, **1988**.

THE pattern of play is laid down at Liverpool and all the players have to do is conform to it. It's a simple formula. Pass the ball to a red shirt and move. If you lose the ball work twice as hard as the opposition to get it back.

ALAN KENNEDY, ex-European Cup winner with Liverpool, **1988**.

IT is a great shame, because they are such a fine team. But Heysel was more than a great shame.

HANS BANGERTER, UEFA secretary, on Liverpool's European exile, **1988**.

I can understand why clubs go away from here biting their tongues and choking on their own vomit, knowing they've been done by referees. In this intimidating atmosphere, you need a miracle to win.

ALEX FERGUSON, Manchester United manager, after 3–3 draw at Anfield, **1988**.

YOU have to say they've been aided by the poorest First Division I have seen in all my years in football.

BOB PAISLEY, director and ex-manager on Liverpool's 29-game unbeaten start to 1987–88.

THE Liverpool side of today is great only in terms of its rivals – there's absolutely no way they compare with the great sides of the past. They wouldn't live with Leeds . . .

EAMON DUNPHY, **1988**.

PEOPLE should ask where were the wonder boys of Liverpool. Why didn't they turn it on when things started to go against them? But then, they have never played well against us. They are good, but not that good.

LAWRIE SANCHEZ, Wimbledon match-winner, after FA Cup final, **1988**.

IT's remarkable how quickly injuries respond up here. Is it the physio, or is it the fear of going out of this side?

BOBBY GOULD, Wimbledon manager, **1988**.

WE may be in the same division as Liverpool, but we're trying to do different things. There are two leagues in one division.

LENNIE LAWRENCE, Charlton manager, **1988**.

WHEN I made my comments about the First Division not being as good as it used to be, it was because I was looking at our own players. I felt there were three or four who weren't as good as those we've had in the past.

PAISLEY, **1988**.

Manchester City

THERE is no limit to what this team can achieve. We will win the European Cup. European football is full of cowards and we will terrorize them with our power and attacking football.

MALCOLM ALLISON after Manchester City's **1968** League championship. City lost to Fenerbahce (Turkey) in the first round in 1968–69.

THERE are three types of Oxo cubes. Light brown for chicken stock, dark brown for beef stock, and light blue for laughing stock.

TOMMY DOCHERTY, **1988**.

Manchester United – 'The Babes'

IN all modesty, my summing-up of 1955–56 and 1956–57 must be that no club in the country could live with Manchester United.

MATT BUSBY in *My Story*, **1957**.

MAYBE we weren't the greatest team in the world. We may never have become the greatest. But we were certainly the most loved. The team had youth, glamour and, above all, modesty. Just as at Liverpool now, the players carried their fame well. The magic of United could have died at Munich, but the emotions that team aroused still draw in the crowds 20 years after the last championship.

HARRY GREGG, United goalkeeper at time of the Munich air crash, **1988**.

I may be thought odd, but when I think of Manchester United, I think of Roger Byrne, Duncan Edwards and Eddie Colman before the crash, and of Harry Gregg, Bill Foulkes and Nobby Stiles afterwards. Best, Law and Crerand were replaceable somehow. They weren't the heart of the team.

BOBBY CHARLTON, **1972**.

Manchester United 1980s

UNITED have begun to think that 'class' is something which comes with big office suites and flash motor cars. . . . That great club is slowly being destroyed. And I blame one family for the ruin. The Edwards family. The master butchers of Manchester.

HARRY GREGG, former United goalkeeper, after his sacking by the club, **1981**.

UNITED keep trying to match Liverpool in the championship but, psychologically, they're just not geared for it. The Old Trafford filmstar image works against them. They're not made to be champions.

JIMMY CASE, Southampton and ex-Liverpool midfielder, **1987**.

THEY are a couple of players short, and one or two of those they've got need a talking to.

BOB PAISLEY, Liverpool director, **1988**.

Millwall

WE'RE regarded as a small club, but we're not. We're really a big club that had fallen into almost terminal decline.

REG BURR, Millwall chairman, before the opening game in the First Division, **1988**.

IF we go to Liverpool next season, we won't be going out with autograph books.

JOHN DOCHERTY, manager, as promotion to First Division beckoned, **1988**.

WE have some players who aren't comfortable of getting it and playing it in their own half, so we try to play our football in the other side's half.

FRANK MCLINTOCK, Docherty's deputy, **1988**.

LET 'em come, let 'em come, let 'em come,
Let 'em all come dahn to the Den!

RECORD played before Millwall home matches.

Moscow Dynamo 1945

I count myself fortunate to have seen Moscow Dynamo twice during their short tour of Britain. Especially fortunate in seeing their brilliant display in the opening match against Chelsea. It was about the finest exhibition I have seen in Britain since the Corinthians were a great side; classic combination and teamwork; superb ball control – the true Corinthian style, now called the Scottish style.

SIR GODFREY INCE, captain of London University team to Moscow in **1914**.

THE speed of the Russian players and the brilliance of their football showed just how far our players had gone back during the war, but this Moscow Dynamo team was a club in name only. The players had been specially assembled from four towns, were the pick of the players from the whole of Russia, and had been drilled into a brilliant machine sent to this country on a political mission with orders that they must not fail.

TOM WHITTAKER, ex-Arsenal manager, in *Tom Whittaker's Arsenal Story*, **1958**.

Partick Thistle

FOR years I thought the club's name was Partick Thistle Nil.

BILLY CONNOLLY, comedian, **1980s**.

Queen's Park 1870–80s

SURELY the greatest of all clubs! I have a great admiration, a great respect, a great esteem – nay, even a great affection for the Queen's Park club. What pigmies some of our strictly modern clubs seem, how thin and poor their records, when a comparison is instituted between them and Queen's Park! What a halo of romance and glory surrounds the Queen's Park club! What a wealth of honourable tradition is theirs!

WILLIAM MCGREGOR, founder of the Football League, in Pickford and Gibson, **1906**.

Rangers Post-War

ALL that running we did. No wonder they encouraged the big men. The dressing room was built for them – we used to laugh because little Willie Henderson had to jump up to reach his peg. When I was there the defenders were men like Bobby Shearer, who was built like a tree trunk.

WILLIE STEVENSON, Rangers and Liverpool wing-half in the 1950s and 1960s, in Motson and Rowlinson, *The European Cup 1955–80*, **1980**.

RANGERS like the big, strong, powerful fellows, with a bit of strength and solidity in the tackle rather than the frivolous, quick-moving stylists like Jimmy Johnstone, small, tiptoe-through-the-tulips type of players who excite the people.

WILLIE WADDELL, manager, **1972**.

Rangers late 1980s

IT's brilliant – now we can beat Rangers *and* England at the same time.

CELTIC fan after another English signing by Graeme Souness, **1987**.

WHAT is it about Souness? Is he still trying to play the hard man? Ranger's disciplinary record isn't just a talking point or a problem. It's inexcusable, unacceptable, an utter disgrace.

BRIAN CLOUGH, **1988**.

IT's too easy to simply say Rangers should go out and sign Catholic players. Who says they want to play for the club?

JIM MCLEAN, Dundee United manager, in *Jousting with Giants*, **1987**.

Real Madrid 1955–60

To be honest I was terribly pleased I wasn't playing. I saw di Stefano and these others, and I thought these people just aren't human. It's not the sort of game I've been taught.

BOBBY CHARLTON on watching Real Madrid *v* Manchester United, European Cup semi-final, **1957**, in Motson and Rowlinson, *The European Cup 1955–80*.

THE best I ever saw, apart from Brazil.

JUST FONTAINE, Reims and France centre-forward, as above.

WE never had a blackboard, and hardly ever talked about our opponents, and this attitude helped us to turn games our way. In the days of di Stefano we just came to the stadium, put on our shirts and played.

FRANCISCO GENTO, Real winger, as above.

THERE was no doubt that they were a good side, but they could be a big naughty at times, and that includes di Stefano.

JOHN BERRY, Manchester United winger, as above.

THEY could dish out the hard stuff too, especially Santamaria. People gloat about them and say they never kicked anybody. Well, they certainly kicked me.

JOHN CHARLES, Juventus centre-forward.

STEVENSON, refusing to believe a team which had put twelve goals past his side [Rangers] could possibly lose, immediately put £5 on Eintracht to beat Real at Hampden.

MOTSON AND ROWLINSON *The European Cup 1955–80*. Real won 7–3 in the 1960 final.

Republic of Ireland late 1980s

IF you have a fortnight's holiday in Dublin you qualify for an Eire cap.

MIKE ENGLAND, Wales manager, **1986**.

PRESSURE? We all feel the pressure, Everyone is human – even the Irish.

RINUS MICHELS, Holland manager, at European Championship finals, **1988**.

I know the way I don't want them to play, but I also know the way I want them to play. I think they might play the way I want them to play if I don't say too much.

JACK CHARLTON, manager, on his Irish side, the surprise packet of the European finals, **1988**.

PLAYING for Liverpool and Ireland could hardly be more different. At Liverpool I do most of my work in the penalty area. For Ireland, when you're not chasing and closing down defenders, you're chasing the long ball over the top.

JOHN ALDRIDGE, explaining his record of one goal in 23 internationals, **1989**.

MUCH more of this and our legs will be worn down to stumps.

ALDRIDGE on the amount of work Charlton expected of his strikers, **1989**.

Scotland 1928 'The Wembley Wizards'

JIMMY McMullan, captain of the Wembley Wizards team, was asked by a sportswriter after that memorable match if there had been a plan to beat England. Jimmy grinned, and said: 'Aye, we laid down a plan. It was a simple one but a stern one. I told the boys: "Now I don't want any unnecessary talking. Get on with the game and don't talk to opponents or the referee." ' The awed reporter said: 'That was good. Certainly it worked.' McMullan replied: 'Did it heck! Alex James's tongue went like a gramophone from the kick-off.' The reporter asked: 'Did you tick him off?' 'Don't be daft,' said Jimmy. 'How could I? If his tongue went like a gramophone, so did his feet.'

HUGH TAYLOR on Scotland's 5–1 win over England at Wembley, 1928, in *Great Masters of Scottish Football*, **1968**.

Sheffield Wednesday

THE trouble with this club is that they want Savile Row suits at Marks and Spencer prices.

MEMBER of Howard Wilkinson's coaching staff at Hillsborough, **1987**.

WEDNESDAY are very cash-conscious. They like to have everything bought and paid for, everything rosy in the garden. That cannot continue if they want success. They've got to spend big money if they want to attract the best players.

NIGEL WORTHINGTON, Wednesday full-back, **1988**.

Sutton United 1987–89

HE has surprise value. He doesn't always know what's he's doing and neither do the opposition.

BARRIE WILLIAMS, Sutton manager, on his FA Cup 'super sub', Francis Awaratife, **1988**.

CRYSTAL Palace told me I was too slow. My answer was 'Bobby Moore was slow and Franz Beckenbauer wasn't exactly fast'.

MARK GOLLEY, Sutton scorer in Cup draw with Middlesbrough, **1988**.

FORTUNATELY our chaps are proper chaps and they do have some intelligence. Therefore they are able to countenance a multiplicity of set-plays suited to the occasion.

BARRIE WILLIAMS on the theory behind his club's FA Cup win *v* Coventry, **1989**.

How can he [Tony Rains, Sutton captain] judge First Division players? If he had put in a bit more commitment down the years he might have finished up playing in the top flight. Underdogs are underdogs because they are not very good! Every Coventry player has shown more commitment than Rains. That's why they are in the First Division and he plays for a team thirteenth in the GM Vauxhall Conference.

JOHN GILES, after Sutton's shock FA Cup victory, **1989**.

Tottenham Hotspur 1900s

THAN the famous Spurs there is probably no more popular club in England. Did they not recover the Association Cup for the south? Did they not play pretty and effective football? Are they not scrupulously fair? Are they not perfectly managed?

PICKFORD AND GIBSON, **1906**.

Tottenham Hotspur 1950–52

THE great thing we built on basically was accuracy. We had two or three great performers, and we had a lot who were not. But they were all made to look great players because of the system we adopted, and because they played in a winning side.

ARTHUR ROWE in *The Encyclopedia of Association Football*, **1960**.

Tottenham Hotspur 'double' side 1960–61

THE theory that the League and Cup double will never be done in modern times is nonsense. I realize no one has done it for sixty years, but there is a simple explanation for that. No club has been good enough.

MATT BUSBY, after Manchester United had lost the FA Cup final and the chance of the double, **1957**.

THEY'VE become lazy. Our play means a lot of hard work, and our forwards in particular have not been keen to carry on that hard work. There has been a lack of desire for action.

BILL NICHOLSON after Spurs had picked up only one point from three games. The next match was won 5–0. Julian Holland, *Spurs – the Double*, **1961**.

Tottenham Hotspur late 1980s

OVER the years Spurs have been regarded as an academy for skill, spraying passes everywhere. But that's what we did to them – on a hard, bumpy pitch. The current Spurs side can play offside until it bores the pants off people.

BRIAN CLOUGH, Nottingham Forest manager, **1988**.

THEY don't fancy it . . .

BOB HAZELL, Port Vale captain, to his team early in the FA Cup victory over Terry Venables's side, **1988**.

THEY were like West Ham used to be. All fancy flicks and sweet sherry.

PHIL SPROSON, Port Vale scorer.

I have come to Spurs to win the First Division. I need it, I desperately want to do it, and I know it has to be next season (1988–89). I'm supposed to have said it will take three years. That is nonsense. A consolidating sixth is no good to me. I must be right at the top with Tottenham.

TERRY VENABLES, manager, **1988**. Neighbours Arsenal won the League; Spurs finished sixth.

I haven't just signed a player, I've rescued a lad from hell.

BRIAN CLOUGH on buying back Tottenham's Steve Hodge for Forest, **1988**.

Watford early 1980s

WATFORD are setting English football back ten years.

TERRY VENABLES, **1982**.

How obtuse. If Watford could put the game back ten years, it would be in a better state than it is now. There would be no £1 million players and wages to suit, there would be less debts, and more fans would be watching.

DANNY BLANCHFLOWER, **1982**.

IMAGINE Franz Beckenbauer trying to play for Watford. He'd just be in the way.

FRANK MCLINTOCK, ex-Arsenal 'double' player, **1982**.

West Ham United

To be sure they had some of the aristocrat's qualities: indolence and unwillingness to sweat, a reluctance to soil their hands. In a way they were con-men. Like all good con-artists they had a certain style. Their play had a smooth, slick quality; it was seductive. Aficionados often purred at the sight of the Hammers and denounced football for denying the game's prizes to the purists they saw in West Ham. It was true they had talent but so did Leeds and Liverpool. They are the real contenders, the true aristocrats. What West Ham lack are values. When the challenge came, their lack of integrity left them at the mercy of the better prepared, the people who worked at the game.

EAMON DUNPHY, in *Only a Game?*, **1976**.

YOU can forget the purist stuff now. We've finished with that. When people start to compare us with West Ham, that's when we'll start to worry.

PETER TAYLOR, assistant manager of Derby Country, **1973**.

THE crowds at West Ham haven't been rewarded by results, but they keep turning up because of the good football they see. Other clubs will suffer from the old bugbear that results count more than anything. This has been the ruination of English soccer.

RON GREENWOOD after England's failure to qualify for World Cup finals in **1977**.

TREVOR BROOKING: It looks as though your side is a bit younger these days?
JOHN LYALL: No, it's just that now we all tackle.

EXCHANGE between the radio commentator and his former manager, **1986**.

I had a gut feeling that something is not quite right there. Billy Bonds is still playing, and when a 41-year-old is one of your best players there's got to be something wrong.

MICK HARFORD, Luton striker, turning down transfer to West Ham, **1988**.

Wimbledon

AT this club if we go to a game we don't usually have a full meal on the way home, just a snack. The players have to wash their own kit, provide their own towels for training and have to clean their own boots.

DAVE BASSETT, manager of the side who won promotion to the First Division nine years after leaving the Southern League.

THE borstal of football.

DAVE BASSETT, manager, **1987**.

THE only hooligans here are the players.

BASSETT when Dons fans tried to invade the pitch after promotion to the First Division, **1986**.

IT's a bit like being at school with your mates.

ALAN CORK, striker, on Wimbledon's *esprit de corps*, **1988**.

EVERYONE says Wimbledon is a fairytale, a miracle. What fairytale? It was hard work and correct planning.

SAM HAMMAM, managing director, **1988**.

TELL me we're deliberately dirty and you're wrong. Tell me we're tough and you're damned right.

HAMMAM, **1988**.

IT was just welly, welly, welly. The ball must have been screaming for mercy.

RON YEATS, ex-Liverpool captain, after watching Wimbledon, **1988**.

WE will continue to play power football. If teams don't like it we will keep stuffing it down their throats. Liverpool will be practising heading for two weeks before they play us in the final.

BOBBY GOULD, Bassett's successor as manager, **1988**.

WE spent 10 years together building something. Dave Bassett can have a thousand Wembley tickets if he wants them.

HAMMAM, **1988**.

WIMBLEDON will take to Wembley. Once you've tried to get a decent bath at Hartlepool, you can handle anything.

WALLY DOWNES, ex-Wimbledon stalwart, before FA Cup final, **1988**.

I went there once to the dog racing on my stag night.

DAVE BEASANT, goalkeeper-captain, pre-Wembley, **1988**.

LET's get the bastards!

WIMBLEDON PLAYERS' chant as the team walked up the tunnel for the final, **1988**.

I was a bit disappointed. I should have caught it really.

BEASANT on his Wembley penalty save, **1988**.

THE Crazy Gang have beaten the Culture Club!

JOHN MOTSON, BBC commentator, on Wimbledon's triumph over Liverpool, **1988**.

I can imagine the likes of Real Madrid and Juventus coming down to Plough Lane to play us. I don't think they would like it too much.

VINNY JONES, midfielder, on prospects of qualifying for Europe, **1988**.

WIMBLEDON are killing the dreams that made football the world's greatest game.

TERRY VENABLES, Tottenham manager, **1988**.

I could take the average non-League player and within one week mould him into the type of player who could hold a place at Wimbledon. Who wants that? Children can't go and watch Wimbledon, pick out a player and come away saying 'I want to be like him'.

VENABLES, **1988**.

I don't want to keep ramming Wimbledon down their throats, but we need their bottle at Sheffield United.

BASSETT, on the way to relegation with United, **1988**.

IT is indeed a privilege and a pleasure to be entertaining the team that has made the greatest impact on British soccer in the last decade.

THAMESMEAD TOWN FC programme welcome to . . . Wimbledon reserves, **1988**.

THERE is one London club which has got it right. Whatever you think of Wimbledon's style of play, you cannot argue with their results.

BOB PAISLEY, ex-Liverpool manager, **1988**.

Wolverhampton Wanderers 1950s

ON the morning of the match, Stan Cullis sent for me and two of the other apprentices, and told us to go out and water the pitch. We thought he was out of his mind. It was December and it had been raining incessantly for four days. When I watched the match in the evening, I understood what he was up to. The Hungarians were two up in fifteen minutes and playing superbly. It was the best football I have ever seen, brilliant first-time movement. But the pitch was getting heavier and heavier. The mud just wore the Hungarians out.

RON ATKINSON, later to become Manchester United manager, on Wolves 3, Honved 2, 1954. Motson and Rowlinson, *The European Cup 1955–80*, **1980**.

WE won it [the League] in 1954 and again four years later, by playing attacking football, which was my whole philosophy. In the late 1950s we scored more than 100 goals for three or four years in succession. Of course that made us more vulnerable at the back, but that was our style. To win the European Cup required a different style. It required players to go against their natural game, and this I was not prepared to do.

STAN CULLIS, Wolves manager 1950s, in *The European Cup 1955–80*, **1980**.

WOLVES' success does Mr Cullis great credit, but it has also done much damage to the game in general in England because so many lesser managers have attempted to ape the Wolves-Cullis technique. Artistry with the ball is not all-important with Wolverhampton Wanderers.

JIMMY MCILROY, Burnley and Northern Ireland midfield player, in *Right Inside Soccer*, **1960**.

ONE well-known manager from a Midlands club said in the boardroom afterwards, 'Football! That wasn't football. Two of the goals came from long belts down the field by the goalkeeper. They never sign a goalkeeper unless he can kick eighty yards.'

STAN CULLIS on Wolves' 1957 victory over Real Madrid, in *All for the Wolves*, **1960**.

Wolverhampton Wanderers 1982–86

I told them 'I'm glad I didn't have you four defending me when I had my court case. The judge would've put his black cap on.'

TOMMY DOCHERTY, manager, on Wolves' defence, **1984**.

IT's a bit like joining the Titanic in mid-voyage.

RACHEL HEYHOE-FLINT on joining Wolves as public relations officer, **1985**.

I just opened the trophy cabinet. Two Japanese prisoners of war came out.

DOCHERTY, **1985**.

OUR strikers couldn't score in a brothel.

DOCHERTY after his team had scored 5 goals in 19 games during the second of three successive relegation seasons, **1985**.

I tried to sign one of the Vietnamese boat people last week, and he said, 'Mr Docherty, I'd love to join Wolves, but I've left one sinking ship already.'

DOCHERTY, **1985**.

WE don't use a stop-watch to judge our golden goal competition now. We use a calendar.

DOCHERTY on Wolves' goal famine, **1985**.

THERE's basically no difference between the Wolves you see now and the Wolves who enjoyed the heady days of the Fifties. They just happen to be in the Third Division.

GORDON DIMBLEBY, Wolves chief executive, **1985**.

2

Of Managers and Coaches

Life and Work

IT was the worst and best day of my life.

BRIAN MILLER, Burnley manager, on escaping relegation from the League, **1987**.

I won't die at a match. I might die being dragged down the river Tweed by a giant salmon, but at a football match, no.

JACK CHARLTON, Republic of Ireland manager, **1988**.

EVERY dressing room should have a poster that says: 'There is more to life than just football and football management'.

GERRY FRANCIS, Bristol Rovers manager, **1988**.

MY New Year's resolution is not to stop in football too long.

FRANCIS, **1988**.

YOU wouldn't treat a dog the way I've been treated.

JOHN BOND on leaving Birmingham manager's job, **1987**.

THIS is not a real job for me. It's hardly a 'get up at six, be at the factory by seven' existence. I loved to play the game, now I love to watch it – and they pay me for it.

GARRY PENDREY, Birmingham manager, **1988**. Pendrey was sacked a year later.

ALL managers are frustrated players.

JOE MERCER, who managed numerous clubs in **1950/70s**.

THE manager's job in those days was to assemble a good team. Once he had done that he just let them go out and play. There was none of this blackboard nonsense you hear about today. Team talk? Johnny [Cochrane, the manager] used to stick his head around the dressing-room door just before a match, smoking a cigar and smelling of whisky, and ask, 'Who are we playing today?' We'd reply, 'Arsenal, boss,' and he'd just say, 'Oh well, we'll piss that lot,' before shutting the door and leaving us to it.

RAICH CARTER, on playing for Sunderland in the **1930s**.

[A manager] is there to be seen and exposed to his players. They will know him within seven days. They will sort out his strengths and weaknesses immediately.

EAMON DUNPHY in *Only a Game?*, **1976**.

GREAT teams don't need managers. Brazil won the World Cup [in 1970] playing exhilarating football, with a manager they'd had for three weeks. Now what influence can a man have who's only been with them for that length of time? What about Real Madrid at their greatest? You can't even remember who the manager was.

DANNY BLANCHFLOWER, **1972**.

A manager's aggravation is self-made. All a manager has to do is keep eleven players happy – the eleven in the reserves. The first team are happy because they are in the first team.

RODNEY MARSH, **1972**.

LOTS of times managers have to be cheats and conmen. We are the biggest hyprocrites. We cheat. The only way to survive is by cheating.

TOMMY DOCHERTY, **1979**.

LOYALTY and respect seem old-fashioned words nowadays, but, as far as professional football is concerned, these are still the most important qualities of all in my view.

DON REVIE as England manager in **1975** – two years before leaving the job for Dubai – in *FA Book of Soccer*.

I was bitterly disappointed about not becoming a manager or coach. Now I'm greatly relieved I didn't, because what's happened since makes the manager even more craven and servile. Outside the half-dozen wealthy clubs, no intelligent, independent-minded human being would want to be a manager in England today.

EAMON DUNPHY, **1988**.

PEOPLE think it's all the good life managing a First Division club. But it doesn't feel glamorous driving from Newcastle to my home at Oxford on a Saturday when we've just lost. The only stop is for fish and chips at Wetherby. Mind you, they're good fish and chips.

JIM SMITH, Newcastle manager, **1989**.

AT Oxford it took me weeks to convince the man on the gate that I was the manager. He always gave me the third degree before he let me in.

JIM SMITH, **1988**.

I'M not just the manager – to save money I'm trainer, coach and physio too, though I have a bloke who does the sponge for me on Saturdays.

PETER MADDEN on life with Rochdale, **1981**.

WHEN I'm doing an ingrowing toenail operation I find my patients talking to me and I'm not listening. At the end I say 'I'm very sorry, Mrs Kirk, I was away – I was just picking the side for Saturday.'

NEIL WARNOCK, Scarborough's chiropodist-manager, **1987**.

BEFORE City scored we could have been 3–0 up. We were playing so well I turned to our physio and said, 'I think I'll have a cigar – if we keep this up we'll get double figures.'

MALCOLM MACDONALD, Huddersfield manager, after 10–1 defeat by Manchester City, **1987**.

ON days like this you get a definite impression that someone up there likes you.

JACK CHARLTON, Republic of Ireland manager, after beating England 1–0 in Stuttgart, **1988**.

WITH our luck one of our players must be bonking a witch.

KEN BROWN, Norwich manager, **1987**.

WE need 20 points from our last four games.

MARK LAWRENSON, Oxford manager, facing relegation, **1988**.

I had tough times with relegation seasons at Sheffield United and Aston Villa. The Villa were relegated and the same day I received a telegram from a Sheffield United supporter that said: 'Congratulations. You have done it again'.

JOE MERCER, **1988**.

IT's the first time I've had two sets of supporters shouting for me to get out.

JOHN HOLLINS after Swindon's Simod Cup humbling of Chelsea, **1988**.

I still think I could be a big asset to the club [Norwich], but I won't be prepared to sweep the terraces.

KEN BROWN on the forlorn campaign to reinstate him as manager, **1987**.

I sulked for three months last year after we lost the (GM Vauxhall Conference) title. It'll take longer this time.

BARRY FRY, Barnet manager, after Lincoln emulated Scarborough in beating his team to promotion, **1988**.

I don't know whether to go out and get drunk or throw myself in the nearest canal.

IAN MCNEILL, Shrewsbury manager, after FA Cup humiliation by League's bottom club, Colchester, **1989**.

WE had no kit, no balls, no towels. My credit card has taken a bashing, I can tell you. After a month in the job I have to keep telling myself that this was better than being a ball boy at Charlton – but there are times when it's difficult to convince myself.

BRIAN EASTICK, Newport County manager, as club slid towards non-League football, **1988**.

HE's scored six goals in about the last 13 games, which isn't bad going at a club like Charlton. We don't create seven or eight chances every game you know.

LENNIE LAWRENCE, Charlton manager, defending his record signing, Andy Jones, **1988**.

IT's a bit disheartening when you are supposed to be a First Division club and you know they get bigger gates in the Fourth.

LAWRENCE, **1988**.

IT's like the Second or Third Division, but with gates of 25,000 every week. At ten to three at Leicester you used to wonder if the match was really on. Here the excitement builds up all day.

GORDON MILNE, Besiktas (Istanbul) manager, on football in Turkey, **1988**.

LAST Christmas I was general manager at Filbert Street. No problems, no-one shouting at me – and no satisfaction.

MILNE, **1988**.

I feel 10 times worse than when we lost 4–1 to Reading in the Simod Cup final. This was the greatest win in my time at Luton yet I couldn't even smile at the photographers.

RAY HARFORD, Luton manager, after Littlewoods Cup final victory over Arsenal, **1988**.

WHEN I arrived in the summer, one of my predecessors told the Spanish press that Meester Terry would be gone by Christmas, but he forget to say which year.

TERRY VENABLES, Barcelona manager, **1984**.

I can still go out as long as it's after midnight, I'm wearing dark glasses and it's a dimly lit restaurant.

VENABLES, during the bad run at Barcelona that led to his dismissal, **1987**.

WE just went out and played the same stale cheese.

FRANZ BECKENBAUER on a poor display by his West Germany side, **1988**.

IF, after 17 years, I get a team to play like that, I have to ask if there is something wrong with me.

GRAHAM TAYLOR, Aston Villa manager, after home defeat by Charlton, **1989**.

IT'S easy to do it at home to York, but can they do it at Mansfield next week when there are coal-heaps all over the place and it's pissing down with rain?

IAN BRANFOOT, Reading manager, after victory over Fourth Division leaders York, **1984**.

ANYONE can intellectualize about what is aesthetically acceptable football. If I had the world's best XI I would tell them to go out and play, win 28–0 and do it nicely.

HOWARD WILKINSON, on his first day as Leeds manager, **1988**.

IF the manager keeps saying, 'We'll win it, we'll win it, we'll win it,' eventually they believe you.

ALLY MaCLEOD, Scotland manager, before World Cup finals, **1978**.

WE looked bright all week in training, but the problem with football is that Saturday always comes along.

KEITH BURKINSHAW, Spurs manager, **1983**.

I am grateful to my father for all the coaching he did *not* give me.

FERENC PUSKAS, **1961**.

SOME of the jargon is frightening. They talk of 'getting round the back' and sound like burglars. They say 'You've got to make more positive runs' or 'You're too negative'. That sounds as though you're filling the team with electricians. But people talk like this without real depth or knowledge of what they're really talking about.

BOB PAISLEY, **1980**.

WE were getting a certain type of manager coming into the game. They were being turned out like Ford Fiestas. They produced a couple of coaching badges and called themselves managers.

BRIAN CLOUGH in tribute to Bob Paisley, **1983**.

RECENTLY my coach underwent a course on Attacking Football run by the FA. He didn't see a goal scored during the whole week.

ALEC STOCK, Fulham manager, **1973**.

EVERYWHERE I go there are coaches. Schoolmasters telling young boys not to do this and not to do that and generally scaring the life out of the poor little devils. Junior clubs playing with sweepers, one and a half men up front, no wingers, four across the middle. They are frightened to death of losing, even at their tender age, and it makes me cry.

ALEC STOCK in *A Little Thing Called Pride*, **1982**.

I'M not a great believer in stereotyped players. You know, A gives it to B who gives it to C, who is supposed to slot it in. I always say to the coaches: 'Yes, but sometimes it rains.' They don't understand me.

MAURICE EVANS, Oxford manager, **1988**.

IF one day the tacticians reached perfection, the result would be a 0–0 draw – and there'd be nobody there to see it.

PAT CRERAND, Manchester United and Scotland midfield player, **1970**.

I sat in my car one day, first in line when the lights changed. I stopped and instinctively everyone behind stopped in sequence. I realized that football was that simple. My team played a marvellous eight-man move last week and one of the kids shouted, 'Traffic Lights'. I could have kissed him.

ALAN BALL, Portsmouth youth coach, **1983**.

I thought it was because I played like 'Pop' Robson, but I soon learned it was because they felt I was old enough to be their grandfather.

DAVID WILLIAMS, Norwich coach, on his nickname 'Pop', **1988**.

YOU'RE welcome to my home phone number, gentlemen. But please remember not to ring me during 'The Sweeney'.

RON ATKINSON, to the press on becoming Manchester United manager, **1981**.

IT's bloody tough being a legend.

RON ATKINSON, **1983**.

THE nearest player offside was at White Hart Lane.

JOHN DOCHERTY, Millwall manager, ruing disallowed 'goal' at Arsenal, **1989**.

It was a Limpalong Leslie sort of match.

PETER SHREEVE, Spurs manager, after 4–2 win *v.* Coventry, **1985**.

It was a bad day at Black Rock.

SHREEVE after 5–1 defeat by Watford a fortnight later, **1985**.

What's the bottom line in adjectives?

SHREEVE after home defeat by Coventry, **1986**.

I have told my players never to believe what I say about them in the papers.

GRAHAM TAYLOR, Aston Villa manager, **1988**.

If they play well against us, we go out and buy them.

ALEX MacDONALD, Hearts manager, in John Fairgrieve, *The Boys in Maroon*, **1986**.

These days I need 10 minutes' notice to score.

JOE JORDAN, 37-year-old Bristol City player-manager, **1989**.

For most home gates there are more scouts here than at a jamboree.

JOE ROYLE, Oldham manager, on his young team, **1988**.

I read somewhere that Oldham Athletic have come out of hibernation. Well, that's not true. We have come out of hospital.

ROYLE on his team's recovery from an injury-ridden start to the season, **1988**.

When I said even my Missus could save Derby from relegation, I was exaggerating.

PETER TAYLOR, **1982**.

WEST Ham will certainly know they've been in a match. We're going there to win.

JIM ILEY, Bury manager. West Ham won their Milk Cup match . . . 10–0, **1983**.

I'VE appointed Maurice Setters as my assistant. He's well placed living in Doncaster.

JACK CHARLTON after taking the Republic of Ireland manager's job, **1986**.

THE only market I might go into would be Billingsgate.

LENNIE LAWRENCE, Charlton manager, denying that he planned to enter the transfer market, **1989**.

I wouldn't check on a player I'm interested in under floodlights. He would look better than he really is.

BILLY WALKER, Nottingham Forest manager, **1960**.

I haven't seen the lad but my coaches have and he also comes highly recommended by my greengrocer.

BRIAN CLOUGH on signing Nigel Jemson for Forest from Preston, **1988**.

AGE does not count. It's what you know about football that matters. I know I am better than the 500 or so managers who have been sacked since the war. If they had known anything about the game, they wouldn't have lost their jobs.

CLOUGH, on becoming Hartlepool United manager in **1965**.

IN this business, you've got to be a dictator or you haven't got a chance.

CLOUGH, **1965**.

IF you threaten certain spiv players, you must carry it out and not let them get away with it. A football team only has eleven players. It just needs one bad 'un to affect the rest. In ICI, with thousands and thousands of people, you can afford to carry scoundrels. Not in a football team.

CLOUGH, **1973**.

LIKE Brian Clough I find it impossible to keep my mouth shut.

JOHN BOND, Norwich manager, **1979**.

THE modern player can't think for himself. He needs a manager bawling at him from the dug-out. And we have not won a trophy while I've been out of the dug-out.

JIM MCLEAN, Dundee United manager, on his three-year touchline ban by the Scottish FA, **1988**.

I will not become a bastard. I don't think you have to swear and scream to get results.

JIMMY DICKINSON, on becoming Portsmouth manager in 1977, in Peter Jeffs, *Pompey's Gentleman Jim*, **1988**.

THERE has been less respect from the players, and no manager can work without that.

BILL NICHOLSON on resigning as Spurs manager, **1974**.

I tried to help the younger players, to be friendly and to respond to their demands. But I must have looked and sounded like an old man to them. Sometimes when I got home at the end of the day, I'd think 'Jesus Christ! What am I trying to do? These players are entitled to their own values, but why should I have to change mine?'

DANNY BLANCHFLOWER, on his spell as Chelsea manager in the **1970s**.

WE were ambushing and being ambushed . . . it sharpens your instincts, teaches you survival. I never stood cowards and lazy bastards then, and I still don't.

JOCK WALLACE, Leicester manager and former Malayan jungle fighter, **1980**.

I'VE come from caviar to fish and chips. It's a down-to-earth club with down-to-earth problems and no pretensions or crazy reaching for the stars. At Tottenham you can buy daft. At Leicester I have to buy sensibly.

DAVID PLEAT, on his move from Tottenham to Leicester, **1987**.

NEWCASTLE have the potential to allow me to pick up the 'phone and say to someone like Alex Ferguson, 'I want to buy your best'. I believe that day will come.

JIM SMITH, Newcastle manager, **1988**.

POTENTIAL gets you the sack.

DAVE BASSETT on the need to realize Sheffield United's potential, **1988**.

DUNFERMLINE Athletic had been my whole life, but there is one sure way to disassociate yourself from a football club – and that is by becoming its manager.

ANDY DICKSON on being sacked as Dunfermline manager, **1960**. In Jim Paterson and Douglas Scott, *Black and White Magic*.

I don't drop players, I make changes.

BILL SHANKLY, **1973**.

A manager can smell the end of his time. The whole club reeks with an imminent sacking. Not that they actually say, 'You're bloody fired!' It's all innuendo and muttering – 'things aren't going too well, are they?' But you know they're after your blood – and if truth were told you've already had your bag packed for weeks.

ROY SPROSON, former Port Vale manager, **1988**.

WHAT many managers who have been sacked would like to say is this: 'My club treated me shockingly. The chairman is a stinker – I'd no chance.' But what they say in fact is, 'I hope to stay in football.'

ALEC STOCK, **1969**.

THEY offered me a handshake of £10,000 to settle amicably. I told them they would have to be a lot more amicable than that.

TOMMY DOCHERTY on losing Preston job, **1981**.

I don't drink, I don't smoke, and I'm getting fed up with gardening. I've no interests at all apart from football and family.

GORDON LEE on being out of work after dismissal by Everton, **1981**.

I took over on a caretaker basis initially. They wanted to see if I was any good. But I'm permanent now – as long as we're winning.

MICK BUXTON, Huddersfield Town manager, **1979**. He was sacked in 1987.

THE facts are that I do need a salary.

LAWRIE MCMENEMY, out of management since his 1987 sacking by Sunderland, **1988**.

I think I have the best job in the country.

BOBBY ROBSON, England manager, **1985**.

IF you don't get uptight you are either a saint or you don't care. And there are not many who don't care.

DON HOWE, Robson's England coach, before heart-attack, **1988**.

THE specialists have come up with just one factor – stress. Like many others I play every ball, make every tackle and get uptight during a match.

HOWE, recovering from triple heart-bypass, **1988**.

THEY phoned to ask if they could come to the house and I said aye that was all right, then they told me what it was about and I said they could still come.

KENNY DALGLISH on visit from Liverpool chief executive and chairman asking him to become manager, **1985**.

I stood up and was counted.

ROGER HYND on being sacked as Motherwell manager, **1978**.

THERE are only two certainties in this life. People die, and football managers get the sack.

EOIN HAND, Limerick and Republic of Ireland manager, **1980**.

THE manager who took us to the semi-finals last time [Archie Macauley, 1959] ended up as a traffic warden in Brighton.

DAVE STRINGER, Norwich manager, on reaching the FA Cup's last four, **1989**.

The Boss

Malcolm Allison

I got him back at the wrong time, 10 years after his peak. That was a bit of a dream – if he was No. 2 in 1970, I thought what could he do as No. 1 in 1979? He'd lived a bit of life in between, and it didn't quite work out like that. The ideas were there, but the physical ability . . .

PETER SWALES, Manchester City chairman, **1987**.

Ron Atkinson

As far as he's concerned, he is God. There's nobody big enough to tell him what to do.

MARGARET ATKINSON, wife of Manchester United manager, after news broke of his extra-marital affair, **1984**.

I'VE had to swap my Merc for a BMW, I'm down to my last 37 suits and I'm drinking non-vintage champagne.

ATKINSON on life after sacking by United, **1987**.

ALBION are one of the few clubs in this country that I would want to manage.

ATKINSON on signing a two-year contract in his second spell at West Brom, **1988**. He soon defected to Spain..

I believe there are only a select few managers who can handle the real giant clubs of this world. I happen to be one of them.

ATKINSON at Atletico Madrid, a month before his sacking, **1988**.

I'VE already paid him £250,000 in compensation yet he wants £50,000 more. He thinks my name is Onassis.

JESUS GIL, Atletico president, after firing Atkinson, **1989**.

I want to see the rear of him and let him go to live the life of an English gentleman.

JESUS GIL.

WHEN I was sacked the most respected radio commentator in all Spain called it the 'greatest injustice in the history of Spanish football'.

ATKINSON on taking over at Sheffield Wednesday, **1989**.

Alan Ball

'IT's nice to have you back but don't try to tell me what to do,' I said. 'You may be the manager of Philadelphia Furies but I'm the manager here.'

LAWRIE MCMENEMY, Southampton manager, on Ball in *Diary of a Season*, **1979**.

Dave 'Harry' Bassett

I can still see Harry screaming, 'You're just a bunch of clowns, amateurs . . . that's why you'll never reach the top.' Twenty minutes later, the van chugged to a halt on the M4. Harry had forgotten to fill it up with petrol.

WALLY DOWNES, Wimbledon player in Fourth Division under Bassett, **1988**.

I'D like to think that the players have released themselves from Dave Bassett's shackles. The media bombardment of Bassett was unbelievable and perhaps the players got left behind.

BOBBY GOULD, Bassett's successor at Wimbledon, **1988**.

WHEN Dave Bassett left Wimbledon, Bobby Gould inherited a good set of players and a system which worked well for them. He was sensible and changed as little as possible. When Bassett took over Watford he found himself in a similar position, but tried to change everything overnight. One manager is sixth in the First Division, the other is out of work.

JOHN MCCLELLAND, Watford captain, on Bassett's resignation, **1988**.

THE image I had at Wimbledon was of an ebullient cheeky fellow, and I wasn't the Archbishop of Canterbury that Watford needed.

BASSETT after taking over at Sheffield United, **1988**.

Sir Matt Busby

MATT Busby is a symbol of everything that is best in our great national game.

SIR HAROLD WILSON, ex-Prime Minister, **1978**.

Father of Football.

BOOK TITLE by David Miller, **1970**.

WHEN Matt and Stan Cullis were first building their sides some of us who had been around before the war said to them, 'You're crazy. The young players today aren't any good, you're wasting your time.' But he knew what he was about.

JOE MERCER.

THE great thing about Busby was that you would go in there fighting and full of demands. And he would give you nothing at all. He might even take a tenner off your wages. And you would come out thinking 'What a great guy.' I remember going in there once, absolutely livid. And ten minutes later I came out, no better off, walking on air. Delighted.

EAMON DUNPHY in *Only a Game?*, **1976**.

Herbert Chapman

HERBERT Chapman worked himself to death for Arsenal, and if that is going to be my fate too, then I'll accept it.

TOM WHITTAKER, Arsenal manager, before his death in **1956**.

NEVER have I seen Herbert Chapman look so miserably unhappy. . . . The team which he had made one of the greatest in the history of football, beaten by a fifth-rate side. Napoleon must have felt like that in Russia, 121 years before.

CLIFF BASTIN, Arsenal winger, on Arsenal's FA Cup calamity at Walsall, **1933**, in *Cliff Bastin Remembers*.

HE was not a blustering bully. Chapman, who gave few words of praise and fewer of blame, inspired awe and respect, rather than fear. He had complete command of us all.

CLIFF BASTIN.

Jack Charlton

I will never forget that first team meeting. I sat there with my stomach bulging over my shorts and trying to avoid the scrutiny of the new manager whose eyes were firmly fixed on me as he told us that there was no way he was coming to Middlesbrough to be a loser . . . He then pulled me to one side and really spelled it out. The essence of it was to get on or get out but those who know Jack will be able to imagine exactly how he phrased it.

GRAEME SOUNESS in *No Half Measures*, **1985**.

I told him not to be such a great big baby.

STAN SEYMOUR, Newcastle chairman, on Charlton's resignation, **1985**.

I'M a hero now but I know I could be a bum in a year's time.

CHARLTON, after success managing the Republic of Ireland, **1988**.

Brian Clough

SUCCESS? Tell me that date when my obituary is going to appear and I'll tell you whether I've been a success or not. If I get to sixty I shall have done pretty well.

CLOUGH, **1973**.

HE is a kind of Rolls Royce Communist.

MALCOLM ALLISON, **1973**.

HE has criticized Sir Matt Busby, me personally, Norman Hunter, Peter Lorimer, Billy Bremner, Peter Storey . . . people whose records stand to be seen. He talks about honesty. If honesty is going to destroy the game, you are doing it a great disservice.

DON REVIE, **1974**.

CLOUGH talks in riddles. He says things like, 'If you were half as flamboyant on the pitch as you are off it, you'd be a world-beater.' What good is that?

JUSTIN FASHANU, Clough's £1m Nottingham Forest signing, after being suspended by the manager, **1982**.

A player can never feel too sure of himself with Clough. That's his secret.

ARCHIE GEMMILL, Forest player, in Peter Taylor, *With Clough by Taylor*, **1980**.

I was wrong to sign for Mr Clough. I'd heard of his reputation – but I just don't understand him. We rarely see the manager during the week but we can find him in the papers every day.

FRANS THIJSSEN, briefly a Forest player, **1983**.

I find it ironical that Brian Clough should call for a total ban on TV soccer after making the kind of money as a member of TV's World Cup panel that would seem a pools win to small clubs.

DEREK DOUGAN, former TV panel colleague, **1983**.

I want to be manager of Scotland.

CLOUGH, **1985**.

IT'S easy enough to get to Ireland. Just a straight walk across the Irish Sea as far as I'm concerned.

CLOUGH, confirming his application for the Republic's manager's job, **1985**.

I can't promise to give the team talk in Welsh, but from now on I shall be taking my holidays in Porthcawl and I've bought a complete set of Harry Secombe albums.

CLOUGH on his hopes of becoming Wales's manager, **1988**.

I think the decision the directors have made is as bad as those I made in sanctioning the signings of Fashanu, Ward and Wallace, which could easily have sent this club to the wall.

CLOUGH on Forest's refusal to allow him to take Wales job, **1988**.

I am boiling about what happened today and I'm going home to think about my next move. I'm going to sleep on it. And if I wake up in the morning still thinking of quitting I'll sleep on it again. And if the feeling remains – then I'll be off. No mucking about.

CLOUGH on the Welsh job, **1988**.

I am going nowhere. Resignations are for Prime Ministers and cabinets, and those caught with their trousers down, not for me.

CLOUGH two days later.

I am a bighead, not a figurehead.

CLOUGH on why he has refused company directorships, **1987**.

HE is a genius. I just work hard.

ARTHUR COX, Derby County manager, **1987**.

NOBODY lifted a team better than Cloughie. He has proved that down the years at Derby and Forest. Not to put too fine a point on it he has got blood out of a stone in dealing with some very ordinary players. Yet look what he has done with them – conquered Europe and the First Division.

RON ATKINSON, **1988**.

THE mere fact that he's on the ground will be enough to put the fear of God into his players.

IAN GREAVES, ex-Bolton and Huddersfield manager, on Clough's touchline ban, **1989**.

'I had the reputation of a playboy in London, but a lot of it was paper talk.'
Charlie Nicholas. *Above*, the playboy discovers the bottom line in one-touch
football

'My name is John Barn-es/When I do my thing/The crowd go bananas!' From
'Anfield Rap', a fruitful dig at racist heels

'Today's attendance 22,451 – and 7,000 inflatables!' Manchester City scoreboard, 1989. *Above*, whales carrying blow-up people watch Wimbledon's Hans Segers deflate Everton by saving a penalty

'All those memories. . . . We had to go back, didn't we?' Roger Alwen, Charlton chairman, 1989. *Below*, the Valley of neglect

'Friendly British football fans salute their Albanian comrades.' *Above left*, England supporters' T-shirt slogan in Tirana, 1989

'We're expecting an offer from Melchester Rovers.' Bill McMurdo, Mo Johnston's agent. *Above right*, Roy Race, ageless player-manager, has other ideas

'Favourite food: Conkers in gravy.' From fanzine 'profile' of Wolves' goal-hungry England striker Steve Bull

'I don't know what all the fuss is about. I wasn't even booked.' *Above left*, Vinny Jones, 1988, after squeezing Paul Gascoigne out of the game

'Believe it or not, Vinny is a very disciplined lad.' Don Howe, 1988. *Above right*, a model of modesty and restraint after FA Cup triumph

'In Don Revie's day he wouldn't have got through the door, let alone put a Leeds shirt on.' John Giles on Jones' transfer to Leeds. Giles' partner Billy Bremner, sent off at Wembley 15 years earlier, finds a linesman loath to swap shirts

You'll still hear him in the directors' box.

STUART GRAY, Aston Villa and ex-Forest player, **1989**.

Kenny Dalglish

He'll probably make a better manager than many of those about. He loves football. I see those blokes like Malcolm Allison and Terry Neill trying to fool everyone by putting on a tracksuit, when everyone knows all they really want is a platform for self-promotion. Kenny's different.

TOMMY SMITH on Dalglish's appointment as Liverpool player-manager, **1985**.

He would make a perfect trade union official.

GRAEME SOUNESS in *No Half Measures*, **1985**.

I know he hates me. He's walked past me on the golf course as if I were a tree. He's the moaningest minnie I've ever known.

JOHN BOND, Birmingham manager, **1987**.

I have come to the conclusion that Kenny Dalglish has been put on this earth by God to be a winner at everything. I honestly believe he has been blessed.

DON REVIE, former Leeds and England manager, **1988**.

I don't know what will happen when he goes full-time.

BOBBY ROBSON, **1988**.

Tommy Docherty

All this talk about Tommy Docherty not being fit to run a football club is rubbish. That's *exactly* what he's fit for.

CLIVE JAMES, **1979**.

His interests are limited to say the least. At home he never read anything in the newspapers but the sports pages. His knowledge of what goes on outside football is so restricted that he couldn't understand why he kept getting into trouble for parking on double yellow lines. He thought they were a new form of street decoration.

CATHERINE LOCKLEY, Docherty's daughter, **1981**.

He's gone 200 years too late.

FIRST DIVISION MANAGER on Docherty's move to Australia, **1981**.

TOMMY Docherty criticizing Charlie Nicholas is like Bernard Manning telling Jimmy Tarbuck to clean up his act.

GORDON TAYLOR, players' union secretary, replying to Docherty's remarks on Nicholas's 'indiscipline', **1984**.

The Hurricane Higgins of football.

HARRY GREGG, ex-Manchester United goalkeeper, **1988**.

Alex Ferguson

You might as well talk to my (baby) daughter. You'll get more sense out of her.

KENNY DALGLISH to reporter interviewing Ferguson, after bitter Liverpool-Manchester United match, **1988**.

He's special when it comes to fighting back.

ARCHIE KNOX, Ferguson's assistant at Aberdeen and Old Trafford, after cup defeats by Oxford and Arsenal in quick succession, **1988**.

Trevor Francis

TREVOR is a charming young man. But him in football management? Asking people like Francis or Peter Shilton, who also wants to be a boss, is like asking me to become a miner at 53. I'd be a hazard to my colleagues. Management is that hard – especially for a lad like him brought up on five-star hotels, à la carte menus and vast sums of money.

> BRIAN CLOUGH explaining that Francis was 'too nice' to become a manager with QPR, **1988**.

I don't know what this nice-guy tag means. Do you have to be nasty to be a manager?

> FRANCIS, **1988**.

TREVOR says football is your life. But this is what life's about, not playing 90 minutes as a footballer. We are human beings. There are more important things in life. Now those flowers [sent by Francis] will go straight in the dustbin.

> MARTIN ALLEN, QPR midfielder, after being fined £1500 by Francis for attending birth of his son instead of playing at Newcastle, **1989**.

FROM the manager's chair, players are interesting people. They want everything from the profession. Big cars, best hotels, first-class travel and huge salaries. But they let you down when it comes to the crunch.

> FRANCIS on the Allen affair, after which he said QPR was 'not a holiday camp', **1989**.

Don Howe

IT was like finding Miss World was free and asking for a date.

> BOBBY GOULD, Bristol Rovers manager, on Howe's agreeing to work as his coach, **1986**.

Howard Kendall

THIRTY thousand stay-at-home fans can't be wrong. Bring back attractive winning football at Goodison. Kendall out.

EVERTON ACTION GROUP leaflet, December **1985**. In May, Kendall's team won the FA Cup; the following season they were League champions.

HE became, in the end, probably the best manager in England. But I saw two different Howards. When things were going wrong, he became almost a nervous wreck. Then Adrian Heath scored that goal at Oxford and turned the whole thing around. Howard had great ideas and was a great coach – always in a tracksuit.

JOHN BAILEY, former Everton defender, in Brian Barwick and Gerald Sinstadt, *The Great Derbies, Everton v Liverpool*, **1988**.

Ally MacLeod

I think Ally MacLeod believes tactics are a new kind of peppermint.

SCOTLAND PLAYER, **1978**.

Dave Mackay

I worshipped him until the day he took off his boots. Then the barrel-chested giant became for me a Tom Thumb in management.

BRIAN CLOUGH, **1976**.

HE was harder than Souness – hey, and a damn sight more talented too. What the hell's he doing at Doncaster while Souness is with Rangers?

CLOUGH, **1988**.

Joe Mercer

WHEN Joe Mercer and I were friends no one in football could live with us. Between us we had it all. I charged into situations like a bull, full of aggressive ambition and a contempt for anyone who might be standing in my way. And Joe came behind me, picking up the pieces, soothing the wounded and the offended with that vast charm.

MALCOLM ALLISON in *Colours of My Life*, **1975**.

Colin Murphy (Lincoln City)

HE talks like a product of an unlikely liaison between Stanley Unwin and Mrs Malaprop.

JOE LOVEJOY, the *Independent*, **1988**.

Bill Nicholson

I did not enjoy dancing around waving trophies in the air. I'm sure he did not like it either. His comments regarding success were always cold, much colder than mine. I was embarrassed by the boasting around us, but I escaped it with humour. He gruffed his way out of it. Our satisfaction was in doing the job.

DANNY BLANCHFLOWER on their partnership at Tottenham, where Nicholson managed the 'double' team captained by Blanchflower, **1961**.

Willie Ormond

WILLIE never gave us talks about foreign teams, because he couldn't pronounce their names. But once in Scandinavia he stopped us as we were going out and said, 'Watch out for the blond at corners and free kicks.' So we went out onto the field and looked across at them, and there were about six big blonds. Well, we were playing Sweden.

SCOTLAND PLAYER, **1974**.

Bob Paisley

HE'S broken this silly myth that nice guys don't win anything. He's one of the nicest guys you could meet in any industry or any walk of life – and he's a winner.

BRIAN CLOUGH, **1978**.

Sir Alf Ramsey

SOME respected, knowledgeable observers feel that Ramsey has serious shortcomings as a manager. At the same time there are many people inside football who have enormous, unequivocal admiration for Ramsey the manager. A few find him flawless; most admit he has deficiencies, but some of these consider them unimportant beside his qualities. The same could be said for Rasputin.

MAX MARQUIS, *Anatomy of a Football Manager*, **1970**.

IT is clear that Ramsey is self-conscious to a highly inhibitory degree about his elocution. In public he lets words go through a tightly controlled mouth; his eyes move uneasily. Yet he is to be no more blamed or mocked for his speech than someone who cannot sing in tune. . . . If this were not enough, his words are noted down meticulously and used in evidence against him.

MAX MARQUIS, as above.

YOU must be f—— joking.

RAMSEY, after being told 'Welcome to Scotland' at Prestwick Airport by a Scots journalist, **1967**.

WE'VE all followed Ramsey. The winger was dead once you played four defenders. Alf saw that in 1966 and it just took the rest of us a little longer to understand.

DAVE BOWEN, Wales manager, in Tony Pawson, *The Football Managers*, **1973**.

THERE's no substitute for skill, but the manager's job is usually to find one. Ramsey obviously found one.

GEORGE RAYNOR, in Max Marquis, *Anatomy of a Football Manager*, **1970**.

RAMSEY recognized that the real strengths and values of English football were embodied not by Trevor Brooking, but by Nobby Stiles. Ramsey was right.

EAMON DUNPHY, **1981**.

As a manager, Alf Ramsey is like a good chicken farmer. If a hen doesn't lay, a good chicken farmer wrings its neck.

JACKIE MILBURN, journalist, formerly Newcastle United and England centre-forward of the 1940s and 50s.

Don Revie

HE was an utterly brilliant manager, but knotted with fear.

GARY SPRAKE, ex-Leeds goalkeeper in David Miller, *World Cup: The Argentina Story*, **1978**.

WHEN I was playing there was often very little contact between some of the managers and their players, and in my experience Don Revie was the first man to really get close to his players.

BOBBY COLLINS, Leeds captain in early 1960s, **1988**.

DON Revie's appointment as England manager was a classic example of poacher turning gamekeeper.

ALAN HARDAKER in *Hardaker of the League*, **1977**.

HE was called greedy and deceitful but anyone who knows him knows he's just the opposite.

DUNCAN REVIE on his father, **1987**.

HE's been out of football 10 years but he still stops the traffic.

DUNCAN REVIE, **1987**.

Bobby Robson

HIS natural expression is that of a man who fears he might have left the gas on.

DAVID LACEY, the *Guardian*, **1985**.

I'M fed up with him pointing to his grey hairs and saying the England job has aged him 10 years. If he doesn't like the seat at Lancaster Gate, why doesn't he go back to his orchard in Ipswich?

BRIAN CLOUGH, **1983**.

I went over in my mind my decisions, my selections, my preparations, and everything else that could have contributed to our exit. There was absolutely nothing I would have changed.

ROBSON after England's exit from World Cup, **1986**.

GOING out after a week has nothing to do with bad tactics, bad players or bad spirits – only bad finishing.

ROBSON after England's three defeats in the European Championships, **1988**.

IF it [demands for his resignation] had frightened me, I'd have kept my quality of life at Ipswich. I'd have kept driving my Jag six miles to work every day, and got drunk with the chairman every Saturday night.

ROBSON after England's failure in European Championships, **1988**.

IN England we tend to internalize things. If something upsets us in a restaurant we don't complain; we go home, sprout an ulcer, and blame it all on Bobby Robson.

HELEN LEDERER, comedienne, on TV show *Naked Video*, **1989**.

Ron Saunders

HE'LL never forgive Bob Geldof for thinking of Live Aid before him.

MIDLANDS journalist on Birmingham's manager's Save Our Society campaign, **1985**.

Bill Shankly

I believe Bill Shankly died of a broken heart after he stopped managing Liverpool and saw them go on to even greater success without him. Giving your whole life to a football club is a sad mistake.

JOHN GILES on his return to the manager's chair at West Bromwich Albion, **1984**.

Graeme Souness

WHAT impressed me most was his attitude. He wanted to bring the best out in people.

TERRY BUTCHER, Souness's Rangers captain, in *Both Sides of the Border*, **1987**.

THE gaffer has knocked containers of orange squash flying, brought a television set crashing to the floor and damaged several dressing-room doors in the heat of the moment!

BUTCHER on Souness's 'attitude' compared with his gentler assistant, Walter Smith, as above.

Jock Stein

JOHN, you're immortal.

BILL SHANKLY to Stein in Celtic dressing-room after European Cup final victory over Inter Milan, **1967**.

BOB Paisley was brilliant, but he could not always communicate with the players. Joe Fagan had technical knowledge and could communicate but he got the job when, maybe, he was too old for it. Jock had everything. He had the knowledge; he had that nasty bit that managers must have; and he could communicate. On top of it all, he was six feet tall, and sometimes he seemed to get bigger when he was talking to you. He was the best.

GRAEME SOUNESS, former Liverpool and Scotland captain, in Ken Gallacher, *Jock Stein, The Authorized Biography*, **1988**.

Peter Taylor

I'M not equipped to manage successfully without him [Peter Taylor]. I am the shop front. He is the goods in the back. Peter's strength is that he has the ability to see things twenty-four hours before I do. I like time if the decision has to be right. In assessing a player, for example, I like three weeks. Peter often has to do it in ninety minutes.

BRIAN CLOUGH, **1973**.

WE pass each other on the A52 going to work on most days of the week. But if his car broke down and I saw him thumbing a lift, I wouldn't pick him up – I'd run him over.

CLOUGH after the break-up of the partnership, **1983**.

Howard Wilkinson

HE turned down a job in Saudi Arabia because they couldn't guarantee any hills for the players to run up and down.

MIKE LYONS, Sheffield Wednesday defender, on his manager's notorious training routines, **1985**.

WHEN Wilkinson said last year that Wednesday were just two players away from being a championship side, I didn't realize he meant Maradona and Gullit.

LETTER to Sheffield *Green 'Un*, **1989**. Wilkinson had joined Leeds months earlier.

Walter Winterbottom

BECAUSE I play for England he thinks I understand peripheral vision and positive running.

JIMMY GREAVES, two years before Winterbottom gave way to Alf Ramsey as England manager, **1960**.

I'M as bad a judge of strikers as Walter Winterbottom – he gave me only two caps.

BRIAN CLOUGH, **1988**.

3

The Game That Was

FORASMUCH as there is great noise in the city caused by hustling over large balls, from which many evils may arise, which God forbid, we command and forbid on behalf of the King, on pain of imprisonment, such game to be used in the city in future.

EDWARD II, proclamation banning football, 1314.

No foteball player be used or suffered within the City of London and the liberties thereof upon pain of imprisonment.

QUEEN ELIZABETH I, proclamation, 1572.

FOOTEBALLE is a pastime to be utterly objected by all noble men, the game giving no pleasure, but beastlie furie and violence.

SIR THOMAS ELYOT, 1579.

LORD, remove these exercises from the Sabaoth. Any exercise which withdraweth from godliness either upon the Sabaoth or on any other day, is wicked and to be forbidden.

PHILLIP STUBBES, *Anatome of Abuses in the Realme of England*, 1583. Stubbes, a Puritan, saw football as a 'devilishe pastime'.

THEY have the sleights to meet one betwixt two, to dash him against the hart with their elbowes, to butt him under the short ribs with their griped fists, and with their knees to catch him on the hip and pick him on his neck, with a hundred such murthering devices . . .

PHILLIP STUBBES, on the early art of tackling.

FOR as concerning football playing, I protest unto you it may be rather called a friendlie kinde of fyghte than a play or recreation, a bloody or murthuring practise than a felowly sporte or pastime.

PHILLIP STUBBES.

THAT whereas there has been heretofore great disorders in our town of Manchester, and the inhabitants thereof greatly wronged and charged with makinge and amendinge of their glasse windows broken yearelye and spoyled by a companye of lewd and disordered persons using that unlawful exercise of playinge with the ffote-ball in ye streets of ye sd towne breakinge many men's windowes and glasse at their plesures and other great enormities. Therefore we of this jury doe order that no manner of persons hereafter shall play or use the ffote-ball in any street within the said towne of Manchester.

MANCHESTER LETE ROLL, **1608**.

IN winter foot-ball is a useful and charming exercise. It is a leather ball about as big as one's head, filled with wind. This kick'd about from one to t'other in the streets, by him that can get it, and that is all the art of it.

J. MISSON, *Memoirs and Observations of M. Mission in His Travels over England*, **1697**.

IN cold weather you sometimes see a score of rascals in the streets kicking at a ball, and they will break panes of glass and smash the windows of coaches, and will also knock you down without the slightest compunction; on the contrary they will roar with laughter.

CÉSAR DE SAUSSURE, 'Letter from England', **1728**.

THE game was formerly much in vogue among the common people though of late years it seems to have fallen into disrepute and is but little practised.

JOSEPH STRUTT, historian, **1801**.

PUT out of the game any player wilfully breaking any of the football rules.

HARROW SCHOOL, direction to umpires, pre-**1860**.

A player is considered to be 'sneaking' when only three, or less than three, of the opposite side are before him and the ball behind him, and in such case he may not kick the ball.

ETON SCHOOL football rule, pre-**1860**.

WHAT happens when a game of football is proposed at Christmas among a party of young men assembled from different schools? Alas! We have seen the attempt made again and again, but invariably with a failure as the result. The Eton man is enamoured of his own rules, and turns his nose up at Rugby as not sufficiently aristocratic; while the Rugbeian retorts that 'bullying' and 'sneaking' are not to his taste, and he is not afraid of his shins, or of a 'maul' or 'scrimmage'. On hearing this the Harrovian pricks up his ears, and though he might previously have sided with Rugby, the insinuation against the courage of those who do not allow 'shinning' arouses his ire, and causes him to refuse to play with one who has offered it. Thus it is found impossible to get up a game.

THE FIELD, Editorial, December **1861**.

RULE 3: Kicks must be aimed only at the ball.

J. C. THRING, The Simplest Game (rules of football), **1862**.

BUT why should the Blackheath men insist on hacking? It is clearly an evil, though in some games (the Rugby game for instance) a necessary evil. In any game played according to the new rules there seems no necessity for it, and there will always be enough casual hacking to satisfy the most bloodthirsty man that ever fought for or on Blackheath. Why should not Blackheath effect a compromise, retaining tripping-up, and any casual hack they may get, and abandon all theoretical hacking?

A RUGBEIAN, letter to The Field, December **1863**. Blackheath's representative at the formation of the Football Association maintained that carrying the ball and hacking were vital principles of their game. The club could not join if it was excluded from the rules.

A dangerous and painful practice, very brutal when deliberate and likely to prevent a man who had due regard for his wife and family from following the game.

A. PEMBER, the first FA president, appealing to Blackheath to abandon hacking, **1863**.

IF we have hacking, no-one who has arrived at the years of discretion will play at football, and it will be entirely relinquished to school-boys.

E. C. MORLEY, FA secretary, **1863**.

THEY had no right to draw up such a rule at Cambridge and that it savours far more of the feelings of those who liked their pipes and grog or schnapps more than the manly games of football. . . . If you do away with hacking you will do away with all the courage and pluck of the game, and I will be bound to bring over a lot of Frenchmen who would beat you with a week's practice.

F. W. CAMPBELL, Blackheath secretary, **1863**.

IF anybody thinks I care about shinning, let them give me a kick and try. They'll find it a game two can play at, and I shall not be at all likely to stop and look at the law and see whether shinning is allowed: not I.

We've just been playing a match – it was awfully jolly, I got lots of kicks. It was what we call a 'big little' (i.e. not limited to the crack men) match, and a lot of the fellows' fathers, and mothers, and sisters were there to see. The girls squeaked a bit when they saw their brothers upset, because it is 'in their nature to do so'; but you never hear a fellow squeak even if his leg is broken.

A PUBLIC SCHOOLBOY of the third form, letter to *The Field*, December **1863**.

DESPITE all that has been recently said about 'hacking', 'mauling' and 'shinning', we feel bound to add that football teaches *forebearance*. If, as Plato says, 'a boy is the most vicious of all wild beasts', the taming and training process begins very early and does its work well. We have seen boys playing football resist great temptations and guard lesser boys from wrong. We have also seen them give way to temptation, and manifest immediately afterwards a deep regret and repentance which most assuredly contraverted the Platonian dictum.

JOHN D. CARTWRIGHT, 'Football – The Value of the Game', in *The Field*, October **1863**.

No player shall be allowed to wear projecting nails, iron plates, or gutta percha on the soles or heels of his boots.

LAW 14, Football Association rules, **1863**.

I would earnestly beg all who have any voice or influence in deciding on or forwarding this question to remember that it is the interests of *all* classes of the people, not of the public school boys or gentlemen players only, that have to be considered.

A HALLAMSHIRE MAN, letter to *The Field*, December **1863**, on the great football rules debate.

FOOTBALL is a gentleman's game played by hooligans, and rugby a hooligan's game played by gentlemen.

ANON, though often attributed to an unnamed chancellor of Cambridge University, late nineteenth century.

IT is a good plan, if it can previously be so arranged, to have one side with striped jerseys of one colour, say red; and the other with another, say blue. This prevents confusion and wild attempts to run after and wrest the ball from your neighbour. I have often seen this done, and heard the invariable apology – 'I beg your pardon, I thought you were on the opposite side.'

ROUTLEDGE'S HANDBOOK OF FOOTBALL, **1867**.

THIS club shall be called the Queen's Park Football Club and its object shall be the recreation and amusement of its members.

QUEEN'S PARK, constitution, **1867**.

SHE: I'm afraid Arthur will some day come home with a broken leg.
HE: Don't be alarmed, for if he does it will not be his own.

EXCHANGE between Mrs (later Lady) Kinnaird and Major (later Sir) Francis Marindin, on her husband, in the **1870s**.

CHARLES ALCOCK (Old Harrovians captain): Look here, Kinnaird, are we going to play the game, or are we going to have hacking? ARTHUR KINNAIRD (Old Etonians captain): Oh, let us have hacking by all means.

PRE-MATCH EXCHANGE in the **1870s**.

WHAT has been the recreation of a few is now becoming the pursuit of thousands, an athletic exercise carried on under a strict system and in many cases by an enforced term of training, almost magnified into a profession.

CHARLES ALCOCK, captain of The Wanderers, the first FA Cup winners in **1872**, later the first paid FA secretary.

THE great majority of players were snobs from the south who had no use for a lawyer from Sheffield. The ball was never passed to him and nobody ever spoke to him. . . . They did not understand him and he resented their air of superiority.

SIR FREDERICK WALL, on Charles Clegg's one England appearance in **1872**.

I fear we shall not be able to get up any 'foreign' matches, the good example set here not having been taken up in other parts of the Presidency. I believe the game is being tried in Kurrachee, Scinde, where in winter the climate is cold enough to warrant it; but a three days' journey is rather too much to take for a game played on sand, there being no turf in those benighted regions.

WILLIAM PATERSON (Old Rugbeian), letter to *The Field* on the problems of the Bombay FA, September **1872**.

WE started off in the forenoon to walk to the ground – a distance of nearly five miles; but after reaching our destination found that there was no chance of getting inside the ground unless we paid at the gate. What few coppers we had had among us were gone by this time, and how disappointed we felt, after such a weary walk, at the poor prospect of our getting a view of the game. Just when we had given up all hope, we earnestly begged a cabman to accommodate us on the top of his cab, and it was from that perch I witnessed the first encounter between the two nations.

W. ARNOTT, Scotland full-back, on his visit as a 10-year old to the first Scotland *v* England game in **1872**.

WE are sorry to say that, during a football match played between St Bartholomew's Hospital and the University College Schools on Saturday last at Victoria Park, two very serious accidents occurred. . . . One student had his leg broken, the other his ankle dislocated. It is further stated that others of the competitors were very roughly mauled, especially in the neighbourhood of their shins. Football accidents have been by far too common of late. . . . Rugby, we fear, must be responsible for setting a bad example.

THE LANCET, December **1872**.

ARTHUR Dunn taught us to play football as honourably as the game of life, to recite the Kings of Judah and Israel, to love God and to hate Harrow.

SIR SHANE LESLIE, Memoir of Arthur Dunn. Old Etonians and England player of the **1880s** and **1890s** and later headmaster of Ludgrove School.

IN the North of England . . . the game is often played in a very different spirit, and at times the anxiety to win leads to much unpleasantness.

THE FIELD, **1882**.

AT a cup-tie or an international match, it is quite a common thing to see the Convener of an adjacent county, the city magistrate, the Free Kirk minister, the handsome matronly lady standing side by side with the horny-handed mechanic, the office boy, the overgrown schoolboy or the Buchanan Street 'swell'.

SCOTTISH FOOTBALL ANNUAL, **1880–81**.

THE working population must be amused – is it to be the football field, or the dram shop?

SCOTTISH ATHLETIC JOURNAL, **1883**.

FAN: Is't that t'Cup? Why it's like a tea kettle.
ANOTHER FAN: 'Ey lad, but it's very welcome in Lancashire. It'll have a good home and it'll ne'er go back to London.

S. A. WARBURTON, Blackburn Olympic captain, after winning the FA Cup against the Old Etonians, **1883**.

THE game of football, as originally played at the Wall at Eton, was the author of every sort and condition of football now played throughout the United Kingdom.

THE ETONIAN, November **1884**.

THE admission into the amateur ranks of professional football players is possibly the beginning of the end in an important social movement with which everybody must sympathize. The idea has been to bring together all classes in football and athletics on terms of perfect equality. With the introduction of professionals a new departure is taken. The first effect of the change will be to make the Rugby game the aristocratic one, and the Association game will probably almost die out in the South of England, where it is already declining in favour.

MANCHESTER GUARDIAN, November **1884**.

£1 per week should be ample remuneration for the best professional footballer that ever existed.

FOOTBALL FIELD, a Bolton-based paper, January **1886**.

ARE you all Englishmen? Then I have very much pleasure in presenting you with the ball. You have played a very good game and I hope you will win the Cup.

MAJOR MARINDIN, FA president, to West Bromwich players after refereeing **1886** semi-final *v* Preston, who had several Scots in their team.

THE narrow squeaks that Scotchmen have had in the last two or three internationals have convinced me that English football is now quite on a par with the Scots.

'FORWARD', writing in *The Scottish Umpire*, **1887**.

I believe all right-minded people have good reason to thank God for the great progress of this popular national game.

ARTHUR KINNAIRD, Old Etonians captain, **1874**.

THE professional or semi-professional player does not as a rule delight in hard-charging like the Eton schoolboys, but he well understands the way to bring down his man with an artful trip, while escaping the notice of the referee.

BAILEY'S MAGAZINE, **1891**.

IT was agreed to buy for the players, after the match, half a bottle of whisky and one bottle of port, and to treat the visiting players to a pie and a pint of ale apiece.

FORFAR ATHLETIC Minute Book, **1890**.

SHEFFIELD are beaten already. They are down in the dumps and sitting in the dressing-room quiet as mice. They have not a word to say. They look frightened. But the Rovers are singing and whistling and carrying on like a lot of kittens. Unless I am very much mistaken they will win easily.

R. P. GREGSON, Lancashire secretary, before the **1890** FA Cup final. Blackburn won 6–1.

THE Rangers' football was not lamb-like, which is possibly why the Corinthians enjoyed the game.

C. B. FRY, on Rangers v Corinthians at Ibrox, **1890s**.

MOON had come a long way out of goal and had taken the ball off a forward's toe, and punted it away, and was returning to goal when the forward deliberately assisted him with a distinct hoof. It may only have been the Scotchman's way of showing his appreciation of the save, but Billy saw it in a different light and chased him. The referee saved further bloodshed.

C. B. FRY on the same match.

HE remarked that last year he was in the South of France and one morning when bringing the coffee the waiter spoke to him of the Wolverhampton Wanderers, observing that they were doing very well.

MAYOR OF WOLVERHAMPTON, to the Town Council, 27 March **1893**.

IT [football] does not make trained soldiers of our young men, it is true, but it enhances in them the spirit of pluck, opposition, competition, never-know-when-they-are-beaten, play up Wednesday or United kind of feeling, which tends to the greatness of our national character. Long live football!

FOOTBALL WORLD, a Sheffield paper, greeting the **1895–96** season.

THE artisan differs from the public school man in two important points; he plays to win at all costs and from the nature of his associations, he steps onto the football field in better training.

BADMINTON MAGAZINE, **1896**.

THE tour is ill-conceived. The FA are sending professionals to play against university men.

N. L. ('PA') JACKSON, founder of the Corinthians, on the FA's first foreign tour, to Germany in **1899**.

STRANGE to relate, the professionals managed to behave themselves.

ATHLETIC NEWS report on the tour.

THE team's success in the Cup-ties were appreciated by the public in a way that was, to put it mildly, detrimental to the players, who were encouraged to excess in every direction. Some of the men had not the moral courage to resist this mistaken kindness, and as a result they have had to seek pastures new.

TOTTENHAM HOTSPUR HANDBOOK, **1899/1900**.

'WHERE be bound this afternoon?'
'Gwain to see a football match.'
'Aw. Good match?'
'Us 'ave every reason to believe so. There's a lot of bitter feelin'' between the two teams.'

CONVERSATION reported in *The Cornish Magazine*, **1899**.

THE aggressiveness of the professional element asserted itself in many ways. Not content with almost filling the international teams with professionals, it did all in its power to reduce the one or two amateurs who did play to the level of the professionals. All were taken to the same hotel, all were expected to travel together, and all were asked to feed together.

N. L. ('PA') JACKSON, **1900**.

AFTER playing in a Rugby match some weeks ago I developed an irritable infection of the scalp which has hitherto baffled my doctor, in spite of ointments and internal treatment. The complaint, which is clearly contagious, appeared first in the shape of a small boil, which hardened until a loose crust appeared and this, being dispersed, spread the trouble further. The parts most affected are those which were rubbed in the course of the game. I should be glad to know if I am suffering from 'football impetigo', and if so what treatment should be adopted. I shall then be enabled to enlighten my medico and perhaps benefit others.

RUGBEIAN, letter to *The Field*, March **1900**.

I have just asked one of the Bury players if he was not very tired and his answer was 'I am very dry.'

LORD ROSEBERY, during presentation of the FA Cup to Bury, **1903**.

THE League Committee's decision is to disqualify Christov for a year and let off Sharples with a 'caution'! This year we have Sharples the Throttler! Next we shall have Jim the Stabber and Jack the Ripper! Match reports will soon read like crime records. Will that gladden the hearts of Russian sportsmen? Certainly not. The British, in their typical high-handed manner, with their big voting majority, are banning a Russian who is totally blameless and letting off a man who is obviously dangerous but is one of their own.

MOSCOW SPORT in **1903** after an English referee had sent off a Russian player for a tackle on an Englishman. (The league was made up exclusively of foreign residents' clubs.)

THERE is a daily increasing tendency for clubs to look askance at men who have not a clean record. Clubs have begun to learn – nay, they have learned! – that it does not take many black sheep to lead the whole flock astray. So long as I am connected with football I shall never sanction the admission into any team of a man who has not a clean record. It is all very well to be a fine footballer; but the man who can play good football and is occasionally unfit to do so, is of doubtful value to a side.

WILLIAM ISIAH BASSETT, West Bromwich Albion director and former England winger, in 'The Day's Work: How the Professional Footballer is Trained', *The Book of Football*, **1906**.

I do not like to see footballers getting £4 a week – or even £3, if you like – slouching about in mufflers and dispensing with collars. It brings the game into contempt with the very class we want to draw to our matches.

BASSETT, as above.

THEIR football, although of a different type, may have been equally fine, but underlying it has been the thought that it was a business first and a pleasure second. It is human nature that it should be so.

THE TIMES, contrasting the great professional clubs with the Corinthians, **1909**.

CONSTANT practice, and the living of a strictly temperate life, go to make not only the skilful but the enduring footballer.

BASSETT in *The Book of Football*, **1906**.

'SY, Bill, where's this 'ere Bury wot's playing Sahth-ampton?' It was a Cockney lad who asked the question of his mate as he gazed in wonder on the enthusiastic mob of Lancashire men swarming up the Strand. Bill had to confess ignorance of the precise geographical position of the place in question, and the nearest he could hazard was 'Dahn norf somewheres.'

WILLIAM PICKFORD and ALFRED GIBSON, on the 1900 FA Cup final, *Association Football and the Men who Made It*, **1906**.

GOALKEEPERS do not grow on trees. That is a truism, no doubt, yet many people imagine that custodians of the sticks are as plentiful as berries in autumn.

J. W. ROBINSON, 'How to Keep Goal' in Pickford and Gibson, **1906**.

IN the last dozen years there has been a great change in the character of the paid player. . . . We now see him able to take his position in the best of company, and would have no hesitation in asking a lady to take a seat with him in his saloon. Why, it is a fact that the Manchester City team on our recent journey to London for the final of the English Cup, surprised the occupants of a station they were leaving by singing, and that too quite musically, 'Lead, Kindly Light'.

WILLIAM (BILLY) MEREDITH, 'Impressions of Wing Play' in Pickford and Gibson, **1906**.

IN answer to Berks & Bucks FA, the Council decided that there could be no objection to a player with a wooden leg taking part in the game, provided he did not play in a manner dangerous to his opponents.

MINUTE 21 of FA Council meeting, March **1907**.

DON'T think because you are on the stand you have a right to shout instructions at the players. They know what to do without any assistance from you.

Don't snap your neighbour's nose off because he thinks different-ly from you. You have come to see your side win, and he has perhaps come to see the other.

Don't make yourself a nuisance to those around you by continu-ally bellowing at the top of your voice, it gets on people's nerves and takes away a lot of the enjoyment of the game, besides making yourself look ridiculous.

SHEFFIELD UNITED programme, October **1907**.

THE Football Association is composed of autocrats who demand that we shall surrender our rights of citizenship. We must not go to law without first obtaining permission, they themselves clinging like limpets to the privilege of suspending and punishing us – without allowing us to appear and plead our case before them.

WILLIAM (BILLY) MEREDITH, *The Clarion*, **1909**.

IF William (Billy) Meredith thinks the public are with the Players' Union he is sadly mistaken. I come across very few who do not think footballers are amply paid at £4 a week . . .

C. E. SUTCLIFFE, *Athletic News*, March **1909**, on proposed players' strike.

> HAN we lost afore we'en started?
> Han we heck! We'st win today!
> We'en a team of gradely triers –
> As they fund deawn Ashton road
> An' fro' th' top o' th' League to th' bottom
> We're noan as feeart as what they're coed.

POEM welcoming Newcastle to Boundary Park for Oldham's first home match in the First Division, **1910**.

WERE cricket and football abolished, it would bring upon the masses nothing but misery, depression, sloth, indiscipline and disorder.

LORD BIRKENHEAD, *Pastime*, **1911**.

IT is to be hoped that the picture of two detestable young women wearing stuffed robins in their hats as a 'compliment' to the Swindon football team is a libel and an invention. The footballers who call themselves by the name of our popular little red-breast can hardly be gratified by seeing the dead bodies of their mascot stuck on girls' heads; and if they possess the ordinary, healthy instinct of young Englishmen are more likely to hiss the wearers off the ground than to wish to walk out with them on Sunday.

(MISS) L. SARDINER, Secretary, Royal Society for the Protection of Birds, in letter to the *Swindon Evening Advertiser*, **1912**.

[DAVID] Harvie left Rovers under something of a cloud when it was claimed that he had sold his landlady's piano without permission.

MIKE JAY, author, *Bristol Rovers: A Complete Record 1883–1987*, **1987**.

THE clubs and their supporters have seen the Cup played for, and now it is their duty to join with each other and play a sterner game for England.

LORD DERBY, presenting FA Cup to Sheffield United, **1915**.

Now then my man, we want none of that [swearing].
Thee! Thee fuck off!

EXCHANGE between A. G. Baiche Bower, the last amateur to captain England, and his left-back, Bill Ashurst, during England *v* Wales match, **1925**.

FATHER says I am too smart at multiplication to make a good goalkeeper. Teacher says there is no disgrace in it. . . . I am expecting a gold watch from Miss Cicely Courtneidge, the actress, being the boy who has let more goals pass him than anyone else we know of.

DONALD MATTHEWS PRATLEY, aged twelve, goalkeeper for Raglan Elementary School, North London. **1929**. Raglan's record was played 20, lost 20: goals for 6, against 269.

THE outcry against inflated transfer values has been loud and long and some of the loudest have been foremost in the open cheque rush. It is proverbially better to practise than to preach.

CHELSEA programme **1926–27** – a dig at Arsenal, who had called for a limit on fees but spent £25,000 in two years.

IF insanity is to continue in this matter, then we will be insane with the rest.

ARSENAL programme editorial, **1931**, after reproach by Chelsea over spiralling transfer fees.

I cannot consider the game of football at all gentlemanly; after all, the Yorkshire common people play it.

THE OLD ETONIAN, **1931**.

EVEN then he must have had a horror of professionalism, for as they went on to the field I said, 'Half a sovereign for every goal, Edgar.' 'Money for playing football?' he queried with a frown on his young face.

F. B. DOUGLAS-HAMILTON, on the fourteen-year old Edgar Kail – later an England international though still an amateur – in *The Boy's Own Annual*, **1933–34**.

CLUBS cannot do just as they like – even if they desire floodlight football. That must be in the future. I cannot easily predict an era when the sorcerers of science may easily turn night into day as they now talk to a man on the other side of the world.

SIR FREDERICK WALL, FA chairman, **1935**.

IT is rather old fashioned now, because it was old when I left off 'footer' – 14 years ago – but still, as you know, the old-fashioned recipes are usually the best. Take about two ounces of beeswax and pare it finely into an old jar. Pour on half a pint of neatsfoot oil, and place the jar by the fire. Let the oil simmer until the wax is dissolved stirring all the time. It is then ready for use. The neatsfoot oil acts as a fine preservative for the leather, and beeswax helps greatly to keep out the water. Just try it, boys – there'll be no more stiff boots nor wasted money.

E. W. HARMER, 'Those Football Boots: A Useful Tip', in *The Boy's Own Annual*, **1936–37**.

4

The Beautiful Game

Styles, Standards and Lifestyles

No player, manager, director or fan who understands football, either through his intellect or his nerve-ends, ever repeats that piece of nonsense, 'After all, it's only a game.' It has not been only a game for eighty years: not since the working classes saw in it an escape route out of drudgery and claimed it as their own.

ARTHUR HOPCRAFT in *The Football Man*, **1968**.

MR Lyle Austin, president of the Barbados FA, said at the opening ceremony of the National Youth Tournament that, 'the greatest game brought together peoples and nations worldwide in a peaceful atmosphere when everything else fails.'

BARBADOS DAILY ADVOCATE, 3 February, **1986**.

AFTER being kicked in the back of the leg, YMCA's Clarke cuffed Notre Dame's Hall, at which Clarke's brother pulled up the flagpole on the halfway line and set about all the Notre Dame players. Play was held up 10 minutes while a policeman, the referee, and Randy Harris, secretary of the Barbados FA, sorted out the dispute.

BARBADOS DAILY NATION, 3 February, **1986**.

I'D kick my own brother if necessary. That's what being a professional is all about.

STEVE MCMAHON, Liverpool and England midfielder, **1988**.

I'M very aware of my responsibilities to help younger players and I try to do so by example.

PAUL DAVIS, Arsenal midfielder, in club programme three days after punching and breaking jaw of Southampton player, **1988**.

I like to upset anybody I play against.

VINNY JONES, Wimbledon midfielder, **1988**.

IN open play I don't think I'd use gamesmanship, but if someone went through with just the goalkeeper to beat and I could catch him by bringing him down, I'd bring him down. If I didn't, I'd feel I'd let my team-mates and my fans down.

BRYAN ROBSON, England captain, in David Hemery, *The Pursuit of Sporting Excellence*, **1986**.

IF someone is through and likely to score, then I will definitely upend him. I would do that without thinking. I'd commit a professional foul if need be. If it means me getting sent off . . . and the team getting something from the game, that is better than us getting nothing.

VIV ANDERSON, ex-England full-back, in his biography, **1988**. Anderson was hauled before the FA on a 'disrepute' charge; Robson was not.

THE great fallacy is that the game is first and last about winning. It's nothing of the kind. The game is about glory. It's about doing things in style, with a flourish, about going out and beating the other lot, not waiting for them to die of boredom.

DANNY BLANCHFLOWER in Hunter Davies, *The Glory Game*, **1972**.

FOOTBALL'S meant to be enjoyed and I still enjoy it, but I probably enjoyed it more at fifteen. The finer points disappeared when England won the World Cup in 1966. Now the object is not to get beat at all costs.

ALAN GILZEAN in Hunter Davies, *The Glory Game*, **1972**.

IT is sad, but I no longer enjoy watching football today. Most of the time I find myself looking at my watch and wishing that the referee would blow his whistle and put us out of our misery.

RAICH CARTER, former manager and England international, **1983**.

YOU ought to get a bunch of clowns if you just want entertainment.

ALAN DURBAN, Stoke manager, answering criticisms of his team's negative display at Arsenal, **1980**.

ATTACK and be damned.

DAVID PLEAT, Luton manager, **1982**.

I'VE given him carte blanche, as Ron Greenwood used to say, though I didn't use that phrase in the dressing-room. Told him to go where he likes.

GEOFF HURST as manager of Telford, in Brian James, *Journey to Wembley*, **1977**.

THERE'S no rule to say a game can't finish 9–9.

GRAHAM TAYLOR, Watford manager, after 7–3 defeat at Nottingham Forest, **1982**.

THERE is no FIFA rule that says teams cannot play as they please.

HERMANN NEUBURGER, German FA president, after uncompetitive West Germany–Austria match which took both teams into the quarter-finals of the **1982** World Cup.

IN football it is widely acknowledged that if both sides agree to cheat, cheating is fair.

C. B. FRY, **1911**.

FOOTBALL is a much more cynical game all round.

PHIL NEALE, Lincoln defender and Worcestershire cricketer, **1982**.

ANGELS don't win you anything except a place in heaven – football teams need one or two vagabonds.

BILLY MCNEILL, Manchester City manager, **1983**.

THESE are players; men who play with their heads and their hearts.

FERENC PUSKAS, **1965**.

OUR football comes from the heart, theirs comes from the mind.

PELE on the difference between South American and European soccer, **1970**.

A footballer is someone who can make his feet obey his head.

TIBOR NYILASI, Hungary captain, **1985**.

No footballer of talent should play in the back four.

MALCOLM ALLISON, **1975**.

THE beauty of soccer, the reason why I think it is the best team game of all, is that there are so many factors outside the control of a coach. If a coach could control a soccer game, it would become very boring indeed. In American Football the play becomes just an extension of the will and imagination of the two coaches. This can be fascinating, sure, but I'm not certain it has much to do with sport, certainly as Europeans know sport.

JOHN GILES, Vancouver Whitecaps coach, in James Lawton, *The All American War Game*, **1984**.

FOOTBALL is the ultimate in team sport, and no individual can win a game by himself. Pele is a famous name, but Pele made his goals because another player passed to him at the proper time. And Brazil won games because Pele didn't try to make the goals by himself, but passed to others when required so that the goal could be scored.

PELE in *My Life and the Beautiful Game*, **1977**.

IF I'd wanted to be an individual, I'd have taken up tennis.

RUUD GULLIT, **1988**.

THE world's best eleven players wouldn't make a team. You must have blend.

LEN SHACKLETON, *Clown Prince of Soccer*, **1955**.

FOOTBALL is a simple game. The hard part is making it look simple.

RON GREENWOOD, England manager, **1978**.

A centre-forward should be thinking about goal as soon as he leaves the centre circle, and his shot should be hitting goal as soon as he arrives at the penalty area.

JOCK DODDS, Blackpool's war-time No. 9, in Robin Daniels, *Blackpool Football*, **1972**.

I'M a brave player. A player who isn't brave can't be a good centre-forward. I would be eaten alive if I didn't defend myself.

HUGO SANCHEZ, Real Madrid and Mexico striker, **1988**.

YOU just cannot tell star players how they must play and what they must do when they are on the field in an international match. You must let them play their natural game, which has paid big dividends in the past. I have noticed that in recent years these pre-match instructions have become more and more long-winded while the playing ability of the players on the field has dwindled.

STANLEY MATTHEWS in *The Stanley Matthews Story*, **1960**.

How do I prefer to play? However they tell me – you do a lot for a cap you know. I've played it long out of defence, chipped out of defence, carried it out of defence. And if I couldn't see anyone to give it to, I belted it out of sight. In this game you do what you're told.

JIMMY DICKINSON, Portsmouth and England player, **1940–60s**.

GOOD Continental teams will play football right from their own goalmouth, whereas most teams in the Football League desperately strive to get the ball as far as the halfway line before worrying about a constructive move. Who would deny that we are now not primarily concerned so much about playing football as about preventing the opposition from playing it?

MATT BUSBY in *My Story*, **1957**.

THE Continentals hold that ball, pass it back, sideways, frontways, any way, to deprive the opposition from getting it. We must bring some of their artistry into our more direct game.

DON REVIE in *Soccer's Happy Wanderer*, **1956**.

SOMETIMES I hear old-timers scoff at these blackboard tactics. Frankly I can't understand why . . . in these days of defence in depth and a defence complex which threatens to paralyse all attacking ideas, it is absolutely vital to discuss the opposition; their strengths and weaknesses; and also for your own team to have their own pet moves thoroughly worked out.

DON REVIE, as above, **1956**.

THE Continentals shudder when they think of how football is played in Britain. . . . What horrifies them is the British love of bodily contact, and it is doubtful whether any Italian player would last a season of hard, rugged British tackling.

JOHN CHARLES after leaving Leeds for Juventus, in *The Gentle Giant*, **1962**.

I don't go much for this hugging and kissing in soccer – that's one Continental idea we'll never bring to Upton Park. . . . Another thing I don't like is this Continental insistence on not charging the goalkeeper. Why not? Why should he have immunity?

TED FENTON, West Ham manager, in *At Home with the Hammers*, **1960**.

MY summing-up of Continental football is that they are marvellous winners but damn bad losers. Their acts of sportsmanship are insincere; they play a scientific style of football, it's true, but when we employ similar methods they resort to unfair tactics. We taught them how to play football, but they have manufactured unsporting actions of their own.

BOB LORD, Burnley chairman, in *My Fight for Football*, **1963**.

NOT even in the England team did I ever hear anyone tell us to go out and string some passes together. It sometimes seems that every team game in the world is about passing and possession except English football.

DOUG HOLDEN, Bolton and England winger of the **1950s**.

A pass rising a yard above the ground should be a foul. A player receiving a pass has two feet and only one head.

WILLIE READ, St Mirren manager, during his team's run to the Scottish Cup final, **1959**.

GOAL is the main objective, and theoretically all finesse which entails loss of time or ground must give way as far as possible to forging ahead.

B. O. CORBETT, Corinthians and England player, **1901**.

THIS long game is sheer poison because it represents a complete absence of common sense. You are asking players to whack a ball thirty or forty yards accurately under pressure. Thirty yards, which we set as a limit at Tottenham, was considered rather short. But actually it is very long.

ARTHUR ROWE, in *The Encyclopedia of Association Football*, **1960**.

BALLOON ball. The percentage game. Route one. . . . It's crept into the First Division. We get asked to lend youngsters to these teams. We won't do it. They come back with bad habits, big legs and good eyesight.

RON ATKINSON, Manchester United manager, on the long-ball game, **1984**.

Most of all I wanted to parade my kind of football – the right kind of football – across Europe and beyond. I happen to believe that God gave us grass for various reasons – for cows to eat and give us milk and for football to be played on. A ball looks at its best when it's brushing blades of grass around the world. I don't believe that football was designed to be played in the clouds.

BRIAN CLOUGH on why he wanted to manage Wales, **1988**.

I wanted to establish without any shadow of doubt that Charles Hughes, [director of coaching at the FA] is totally wrong in his approach to football. He believes footballs should come down with icicles on them.

CLOUGH, as above.

I can't watch Wimbledon, Watford or Sheffield Wednesday. Football wasn't meant to be run by two linesmen and air traffic control.

TOMMY DOCHERTY, **1988**.

Because I'm a British centre-forward they expect me to be heading the ball all the time.

IAN RUSH during his sojourn with Juventus, **1987**.

I cannot stress too often my belief that people who talk of short passes and on-the-ground moves as the essence of good football do not help the progress of football in Britain.

STAN CULLIS in defence of his 'scientific kick-and-rush' Wolves, in *All for the Wolves*, **1960**.

It's a big pitch, but with a bit of welly I can still bomb the ball right up there where it hurts.

DAVE BEASANT, Wimbledon goalkeeper-captain, at Wembley before FA Cup final win *v* Liverpool, **1988**.

IF you had players who could fade the ball into channels instead of whacking them, you couldn't half make it happen.

BOBBY GOULD, Wimbledon manager, **1988**.

POSSESSION, patience are myths. It is anathema to people in the game to say this, but goals come from mistakes, not possession.

GRAHAM TAYLOR, Watford manager, **1982**.

YOU play nineteen-twentieths of the game without the ball and that's when you do your thinking. That's when you do your real playing. Any clown can play with the ball when he's got it. It's the good fellows who get into position to receive.

ARTHUR ROWE, in *The Encyclopedia of Association Football*, **1960**.

THROUGHOUT the game we demonstrated the golden rule of modern football; and that is: the good player keeps playing even without the ball. All the time he is placing himself so that when the ball comes to him he is able to make good use of it. We improved the English saying 'Kick and run' to 'Pass accurately and run into a good position.'

PUSKAS on Hungary's 6–3 defeat of England at Wembley, **1953**.

WHEN I returned to the Cumberland Hotel, a small boy came up to me in the foyer and said: 'Please sir, take me to your country and teach me to play football.'

PUSKAS in *Captain of Hungary*, **1955**.

PERHAPS England, once the masters, can now learn from the pupils.

PUSKAS, **1953**.

WE have nothing to learn from these people.

SIR ALF RAMSEY after defeat by Brazil, **1970**.

WE are the best footballing nation in the world.

SIR ALF RAMSEY, two months after England failed to qualify for the World Cup in **1973**.

IT took me sixteen years to realize that this is a passing, not a dribbling, game.

JIMMY HILL, television presenter and former Fulham forward, **1970s**.

WE have learned to bawl 'Get rid of it' just as the mob in the French Revolution bawled 'To the Guillotine'. And our get-rid-of-it addicts successfully sent our soccer to the sporting guillotine.

NEIL FRANKLIN, former England defender, in *Soccer at Home and Abroad*, **1956**.

NEVER try to whitewash British football by saying that the Continentals would not live in the First Division. They wouldn't want to. They prefer to play their football under conditions which allow the game to be played properly.

NEIL FRANKLIN, as above.

WE cling to the myth that our Football League is the best in the world. There are others: the West German and South American leagues for example are as good. But it *is* the toughest in its demands on players and it *is* destructive of national football in its drain of players' energy and in denying them time for national commitments.

SIR STANLEY ROUS, *Football Worlds – a Lifetime in Sport*, **1978**.

IN the last twelve months, going round to League matches, it has been increasingly obvious that skills do not have the chance to develop because of the fierce physical contact.

DON REVIE, a year after leaving Leeds United to manage England, **1975**.

IT is no surprise that England are suffering a list of injuries, because of the impossible strain you impose on them by playing too much football. There is a marked decline between October and April in the performance of your players, and you cannot underestimate the psychological effect of recent club defeats in Cup semi-finals and finals. Such blows to the nervous system take weeks to heal. You are plagued with 'industrial football', yet the potential you have remains enormous.

MILIAN MILIANIC, Yugoslav manager of Real Madrid, **1976**.

THE average Englishman is a limited player.

GLENN HODDLE after moving to play for Monaco, **1987**.

FOR me the ball is a diamond. If you have a diamond you don't get rid of it, you offer it.

HODDLE, **1988**.

UNLIKE the Brazilians we start looking for faults as soon as we recognize a player's skill. I've had it pushed down my throat ever since I was a kid. Of course the runners and tacklers are part of the game, but people don't have a go at them if they can't play forty-yard balls or go past three men at a time. They don't expect them to do the things skilful players are good at. . . . That is the way we are in England and maybe it's part of the reason Brazil do a bit more than us at international level.

HODDLE, **1981**.

THE attitude in England is tricks are okay if they work . . . if they don't you're a wanker. It doesn't seem to have sunk in that if you never try you'll never succeed.

DUNCAN MCKENZIE, **1976**.

BRAZIL played in shoes which could only be likened to Grecian slippers. We cannot laugh even about that. After all, they won the World Cup in them.

TOM FINNEY on the 1958 World Cup in *Finney on Football*, **1958**.

WHILE I was in Rio a photographer asked me to juggle the ball on Copacabana beach. I felt so embarrassed – we were surrounded by kids who could juggle the ball so much better than me.

JOHN BARNES, Liverpool and England winger, **1988**.

I have not seen much of English football, but it seems as if it always has a lot of high balls, strong marking and strong running. Of course, in England football is played on the pitches of winter. It should be played in summer. In Brazil we play more or less all the year round and on some very dry and very bad pitches. But it produces some very good players.

CARLOS ALBERTO, Brazil's 1970 World Cup-winning captain, in **1983** as coach to world club champions Flamengo.

THE older principles whereby success was hacked out from rival limbs are now being discredited in the best circles.

DR PERCY M. YOUNG in *Football Year*, **1956**.

WE have still to produce our best football. It will come against a team who come to play football and not act as animals.

ALF RAMSEY after England's brawl with Argentina, World Cup, **1966**.

IT looks as though brutality pays. Running with the ball, I found as never before that my calculations were disturbed not by fears of a hard, legal tackle, for that is in the game, but by thoughts that I had certain opponents whose chief aim was to disable me.

PELE on 1966 World Cup, in *My Life and the Beautiful Game*, **1977**.

FOOTBALL is not played at top level by a bunch of charity-minded nuns, but the Argentinians are no more dirty or less sporting than anyone else. In any case there are two sides to every coin and if English players or fans think that the Argentinians are dirty players I can assure you that the Argentinians feel exactly the same. Everyone in Buenos Aires is firmly convinced that the dirtiest players they ever saw came from England.

ALFREDO DI STEFANO, ex-Real Madrid, Argentina and Spain, **1973**.

IT was more rugged [in the 1930s and 1940s]. There was more physical contact. We always had what we called the killers in the game, players who went deliberately over the ball to get the man. They were all known, and you took special precautions against them. The play was rougher and dirtier than it is now.

STAN CULLIS, ex-Wolves captain and manager in Arthur Hopcraft, *The Football Man*, **1968**.

THERE were plenty of fellers who would kick your bollocks off. The difference was that at the end they'd shake your hand and help you look for them.

NAT LOFTHOUSE, former Bolton and England centre-forward, on differences between his 1950s heyday and **1986**.

LLOYD McGrath is lucky he's not running in a gelding plate now. That tackle was so high it was very nearly a squeaky-voice job.

JOHN SILLETT, Coventry manager, on challenge by Everton's Dave Watson, **1987**.

EVERY English player autographed my leg with his studs.

GUNTHER NETZER of West Germany after bitter 0–0 draw, **1972**.

ENGLISH football had degenerated to unbelievable levels. The hackers are now completely in charge.

JOHNNY BYRNE, ex-West Ham and England player, **1973**.

FOOTBALL is a physical game. It's about stamina and strength and players battling for each other. A lot of people knock those qualities – but that's what English football is all about.

RON SAUNDERS, Aston Villa manager, on the way to the League title in **1981**.

RECENTLY I went home to England and saw Forest play Villa with twenty players crowded into a third of the pitch, and I wondered, 'Did I really play this kind of football?'

TONY WOODCOCK, Cologne and England striker, **1980**.

OUR failure has not been because we have played the English way, but because we haven't. Bloody football should be honest, open, clean, passionate. Part of a nation's culture, its heritage, is the way it plays its sport. And the English way is with passion, commitment.

GRAHAM TAYLOR, Watford manager, **1982**.

I didn't play in the First Division until I was 29. At first I thought, 'Crikey, how am I going to cope with people like Brady and Hoddle?' But if you believe in yourself, it's possible.

BRIAN HORTON, former Brighton and Luton midfielder, **1988**.

I have yet to see a great football team made up of ninety-minute triers. The 1954 Hungarians, the 1958 Brazilians, and the brilliant club teams like Real Madrid, included many players who would be damned in English eyes for disappearing for spells during a game. Puskas, Pele, Didi and Garrincha all do it, yet each has sufficient skills to win a match in ten minutes, or less.

JIMMY MCILROY, Burnley and Northern Ireland midfield player, in *Right Inside Soccer*, **1960**.

THE World Cups of 1958 and 1962 were garden parties compared with what is involved now, with the pressures that have developed. The increase in pressure seems continuous from one competition to the next. In 1966 it was already terrific, in 1970 it was worse, in 1974 still more terrible and now it is almost completely out of hand. Football has become almost a kind of war.

HELMUT SCHOEN, West Germany manager, during **1978** World Cup.

IT was beautifully done. It was wrong, but it was necessary.

JACK CHARLTON commenting on a 'professional foul' in Barcelona *v* Dusseldorf game, **1979**.

FOOTBALL became popular because it was considered an art, but now too many pitches are becoming battlefields.

SOCRATES, Brazil captain, **1981**.

THE tackling in international football is frightening. Even a nation like the Swiss, not noted for ruthlessness, have joined in.

GEOFF HURST, assistant to England manager Ron Greenwood, **1981**.

No, signor, it is not dancing school.

CLAUDIO GENTILE of Italy on his rough treatment of Diego Maradona in the Italy-Argentina World Cup match, **1982**.

WE need someone to play dirty at times. We missed a player like that in the 1982 finals. Italy, for example, had Gentile, who had no pity when he wanted to hit an opponent.

ZICO, Brazilian midfield player, **1986**.

OF course we cannot measure qualities like intelligence or guts – the imponderables – but we can digitalize everything else from acceleration to accuracy with the help of video recordings.

PETER SONNEMANS, Dutch coach and salesman, trying to sell his computerized measurable training system to First Division managers, **1988**.

CHINA will certainly have a team in the not-too-distant future. They're working on a squad of 100 million kids.

BOBBY CHARLTON, **1988**.

ITALIAN League football was rubbish – totally defensive. Games were either no score, or 1–0. Rarely were more than two goals scored. When we had lost a couple of matches, we began to feel the attitude of the directors. It was as though we had lost a war. Too important! With a reaction like that, players don't want to be adventurous!

DENIS LAW on his spell with Torino in the early 1960s in *An Autobiography*, **1979**.

THE game [in Italy] was like life and death for everybody: for the players, for the directors, for everybody. That can't be the right way. It was not enjoyable to play, and surely not enjoyable to watch, and yet the grounds were always full: which says something about how important the game was to a lot of Italian people. Football was their whole life.

DENIS LAW, as above.

RUSHIE tells me Italians think the Brits are rubbish at defending. But I think it is easier to defend in their game.

KEVIN RATCLIFFE, Everton captain, **1988**.

IF the US becomes enthralled by soccer it will be when every back street and stretch of urban waste ground has its teams of kids playing their makeshift matches, the players claiming the temporary identity of the world's stars in the sport. Environments like that produce those stars. Football is an inner compulsion. It cannot be settled on a people like instant coffee.

ARTHUR HOPCRAFT, *The Football Man*, **1968**.

SOCCER is a game in which everyone does a lot of running around. . . . Mostly, twenty-one guys stand around and one guy does a tap dance with the ball. It's about as exciting as *Tristan and Isolde*.

JIM MURRAY, *Louisville Courier Journal*, **1967**.

THOSE Stoker guys are so cocky they make me mad saying ours is a dull game. Boy, if ours is dull, theirs is even duller. Those nuts. Running around in shorts, chasing a big ball like a bunch of schoolboys.

JOE AZCUE, Cleveland Indians baseball coach, **1967**. Cleveland Stokers were Stoke City.

To say that American soccer is the football of the future is ludicrous. You've got to see football in the black townships of South Africa or Rio before you can talk about the football of the future. I read a lot about American soccer and I still can't name five top American players.

JACK TAYLOR, English World Cup referee, **1978**.

AMERICA is the land of opportunity for soccer.

RON NEWMAN, Fort Lauderdale Strikers' coach, **1978**.

IT's an elephant's graveyard.

GIANNI RIVERA, Milan and Italy, on rejecting an offer from the USA, **1978**.

BECAUSE in this bloody country, Americans think that any guy who runs around in shorts kicking a ball instead of catching it has to be a Commie or a fairy.

CLIVE TOYE, New York Cosmos' British general manager, on why the club gave away so many 'promos' and 'freebies', **1970**.

WITH such refinements as a thirty-five-yard offside law, synthetic pitches which are not conducive to tackling, 'shoot-outs' to eliminate drawn games and bonus points, the country which gave the world Disneyland has provided a Mickey Mouse football industry.

JACK ROLLIN on the NASL in *Rothman's Football Yearbook*, **1979–80**.

TELL the Kraut to get his ass up front. We don't pay a million for a guy to hang around in defense.

NEW YORK COSMOS executive on Franz Beckenbauer's tendency to play deep.

THE indoor game definitely provides more what the American fan wants to see. The outdoor game is better, there's more strategy and tactics. But in America they like a winner and they like action. It's like the ice hockey – I went to a game which was more like a fight and that's what the crowd love. They like the physical stuff.

KEITH WELLER, ex-England player with Fort Lauderdale Strikers, **1983**.

PEOPLE think it's a soft touch in the North American Soccer League but it's hard out there, I can tell you. You travel from one side of the continent to the other, play the next day, fly back and play two days later. You have astroturf and grass and 90° heat with 95° humidity, all these things to contend with. So you can't get away with sitting on the beach and drinking.

KEITH WELLER, as above.

WHERE are we going? What the hell are we doing? Why the hell do these people keep paying me?

ALKIS PANAGOULIAS, USA national coach, on state of soccer in his country before 5–0 defeat by England, **1985**.

MAYBE it's just my paranoia, but I can see newspapers and TV stations running pictures of the Heysel disaster or a riot somewhere and asking people: 'Is this what you want in your back yard?'

JOHN KERR, director of American Major Indoor Soccer League Players' Association, on decision to award 1994 World Cup to the USA, **1988**.

WHEN you talk about international soccer competition you are talking about mayhem, mauling, stomping. First they announce the final score, then they give you the body count.

MIKE ROYKO, *New York Times* columnist, **1988**.

MAYBE it's because it's the only game in which players use their heads to propel the ball. Assuming that the fans of soccer also play the game, all that butting the ball with their heads might make their brains squishy.

ROYKO, as above.

IN England, soccer is a grey game played by grey people on grey days.

RODNEY MARSH, to Florida television audience, **1979**.

IT [Scottish approach to football] stems from a great conceit or, perhaps, a myth, that in Scottish football there is an inspired, spontaneous geometry of purest origin which, when it comes right, will benefit even the defeated. For they could learn from the vision of perfection, a perfection that is of people, made by people, by wee, bitter, narrow, ill-educated men yet full of light and luminous grace.

JOHN RAFFERTY, soccer journalist, in *One Hundred Years of Scottish Football*, **1973**.

STILL the Scottish football ground is the place to go when you're half pissed, to urinate down the back of the man in front of you and to use the language of the barrack room. And, among two legions of supporters in this country, the place to go to sing those hateful songs of Ireland.

IAN ARCHER, soccer journalist, in *When Will We See Your Like Again?*, **1977**.

PRESTIGE is precious to a little trading nation and there is no quicker way to earn it than through football.

JOHN RAFFERTY, *The Scotsman*, **1971**.

WE didn't even have Scotland track suits. We had to bring our own training gear. And what a peculiar lot we looked among the world's best, with the green of Celtic and the white of Preston and the blue of Dundee contrasting with the beautifully turned out teams of Europe and South America. We looked like liquorice allsorts.

WILLIE FERNIE, Celtic and Scotland player, on Scotland's first disastrous World Cup in 1954, in *When Will We See Your Like Again?*, **1977**.

WE were nearly fainting in the heat. But all the advice we remember getting was voices from the touchline commanding: 'Get stuck into them.'

NEILLY MOCHAN, Celtic and Scotland player, on Uruguay 7, Scotland 0, 1954 World Cup, as above.

WE were bombarded with crap about beating the rest of the world into the ground. How could anyone be so optimistic about our chances? When did you last see a Scotland team play really good football, play with positive rhythm and a consistent pattern? It was a fight when we beat the Czechs and a fight when we beat the Welsh at Anfield. Tunisia and Iran are better prepared than we are. In our last match before coming here the lads exhausted themselves trying to beat England. It couldn't be any other way with 80,000 mad Scotsmen yelling, 'Gie us an English heid.'

LOU MACARI in Argentina with the Scotland team under Ally MacLeod, **1978**.

I am proud of my team for beating the best side in Europe. I want to congratulate Scotland for the team they presented to us.

MARCUS CALDERON, Peru manager, during **1978** World Cup.

IF Scotland ever discover that football is a team game, the rest of us will have to watch out.

JOHN ADAMS, FA Northern Region staff coach, **1980s**.

THE Scots are a hard team, and play with excessive violence.

ZAGALO, Brazil manager, on hearing World Cup draw, **1974**.

THEY'RE not so different. They've got two arms and two legs and some of them even have heads.

FRANK 'MAD DOG' AROK, Australian manager, on Scotland team before World Cup tie at Hampden, **1985**.

THE Premier League in Scotland is the most physical, cynical and brutal league in the world. You hear people talking about wild tackling in Spain . . . I don't think any of their hatchet men would be able to live with some of those in our league.

JIM MCLEAN, Dundee United manager, in *Jousting with Giants*, **1987**.

LONDON has become the Third Division city of soccer. No bottle. No class. No chance.

JIMMY GREAVES on the capital's lack of challenge to Liverpool, **1987–88**.

I never fancied London as a footballer or manager. I enjoy it for the odd weekend, especially if it includes a game at Wembley for Liverpool, but that's about it.

BOB PAISLEY, Liverpool director, **1988**.

SIR, Can nothing be done to improve Wembley Stadium? I was there to see England Under-15s play Brazil. As always I was appalled at the shabbiness of the place. . . . If food is to be sold, why can't it be done with a little colour and style? Why is there nowhere to eat in comfort? Why are there so few litter receptacles? Isn't it possible to apply some paint to walls? Wembley is our national stadium. Must it also be a national disgrace?

LETTER to *The Times*, **1988**.

I'VE seen sexier stadiums, more spectacular stadiums and bigger stadiums, but I've been in no other stadium which on the days of a big match has quite the same flavour.

BRIAN WOLFSON, chairman Wembley plc, announcing improvement plans, **1989**.

A vast white elephant, a rotting sepulchre of hopes and the grave of fortunes.

NEWSPAPER description of Wembley at the closing of the British Empire Exhibition in **1925**. (Quoted by David Lacey, The *Guardian*, 1989.)

I don't care how much they are trying to improve Wembley Stadium. The place is an embarrassment. I went through an entrance with a group of Swedish people. Heaven knows what they thought about the place. There was building work going on, I couldn't find a steward or a programme seller. I was disgusted with the surroundings – and I had a complimentary ticket. Those Swedes were paying £17.50.

GRAHAM TAYLOR, Aston Villa manager, on visiting Wembley for the England *v* Sweden match, **1989**.

THE theatre of dreams.

ALEX FERGUSON, Manchester United manager, on Old Trafford, **1986**.

IT's the only stadium in the world I've ever been in that's absolutely buzzing with atmosphere when it's empty and there isn't a soul inside. It's almost like a cathedral.

TOMMY DOCHERTY on Old Trafford, in *Call the Doc*, **1982**.

BLIMEY, the ground looks a bit different to Watford. Where's the dog track?

LUTHER BLISSETT at Milan's San Siro Stadium, **1983**.

TEAMS hate coming to The Den. I remember going there with York City for my first visit. It took us half an hour to find the place. Eventually we went up this dingy back street. I remember thinking, 'Where is this?' Then you go and have a look at the pitch, which is bumpy, terrible. The away team dressing-room is a dungeon, no light, no window. The bathrooms are horrible. Then you get out there to face them – the Lions. And they come storming at you and most sides jack it in. . . . When you have been there a little time, though, you grow to love it. It's one of our biggest assets.

EAMON DUNPHY in *Only a Game?*, **1976**.

THEY did well to get a point. Usually all teams get at Millwall is the tyres let down on their coaches.

TOMMY DOCHERTY on a team earning a draw at The Den, **1985**.

IT's an old stable. Players wash-up in a horse trough. The pitch is a bog, cramped and small. The team play 5–4–1 and that's when they are feeling adventurous. [It's] the sort of place that makes you wonder what you ever saw in football. If the walls of that cupboard they call a dressing-room could talk, they'd spend the first month reeling off the names of those who had lost there and given up the game forever.

TIVIDALE player's description of West Midland League rivals Hednesford's ground in Brian James, *Journey to Wembley*, **1977**.

WE'RE fortunate to have it [the FA Cup] – it's why small boys want to become footballers.

TERRY VENABLES, three weeks before his Tottenham team were knocked out by Port Vale, **1988**.

THIS [cold and damp] dressing-room is our secret weapon for Spurs – not forgetting their lukewarm pot of tea at half-time.

PHIL SPROSON, Vale defender, before Tottenham tie.

I love these derby games. Three tackles have gone in before you can even bring the ball down.

PETER REID, Everton midfielder, **1988**.

YOU always knew it was derby week. The postman would say, 'We'll be ready for you'. And then the milkman would come round: 'You're in for it Saturday.' Then it would be the taxi driver. You never got away from it.

GORDON LEE, ex-Everton manager, in Brian Barwick and Gerald Sinstadt, *The Great Derbies, Everton v Liverpool*, **1988**.

I'VE been as involved as my players in every derby since I've been here. I've kicked every ball, headed out every cross. I once scored three goals – one was lucky, but the other two were great!

BILL SHANKLY before the 1973 derby, rejecting suggestions that he lacked the experience of playing in Mersey derbies enjoyed by opposite number Billy Bingham. From Barwick and Sinstadt, as above.

I absolutely hated them. At that time there was quite a nucleus of Liverpool-born players in both sides, and you could eliminate them to begin with. In our case people like Terry Darracott, Mick Lyons, Steve Sergeant and Roger Kenyon would go about kicking lavatory doors, heading the ceiling and butting the doors. You knew that when you took the field it was going to be a physical battle, a battle of nerves and pride in terms of those five or six players on either side.

DUNCAN MCKENZIE, Everton player, on Merseyside derbies from Brian Barwick and Gerald Sinstadt as above, **1988**.

ABOUT 11.30 we'll go for a walk and then I'll just be wishing it was kick-off time. It's horrible waiting. As soon as I get on the coach I start sweating. My armpits are ridiculous – I don't get nervous before a game, I just start to sweat. I don't mind once I get out of my suit. I'm a bit like a racehorse, I sweat up in the paddock.

PETER REID, before FA Cup tie with Liverpool, **1988**.

IF you can't hit a thirty-yard ball to feet here, you won't be able to do it anywhere.

JIMMY GREAVES on QPR's Omniturf, before the first League match on it, **1981**.

THEY tell me that pitch is where the game's future lies. If that's so, I'm glad I'm getting on a bit. . . . But I was delighted to get a point. Normally the only thing we get out of London is the train from Euston.

JIMMY FRIZZELL, Oldham manager, on the Omniturf, **1981**.

SCIENTISTS are hinting that Northern Europe may be entering a new Ice Age.

QPR PROGRAMME editorial extolling virtues of artificial pitches, during bitter winter, **1986**. The club returned to grass in 1988, leaving Luton, Oldham, Preston and Stirling Albion as the only League clubs with synthetic turf.

IT'LL never replace plastic.

RAY HARFORD, Luton manager, on Coventry's heavily-sanded grass pitch, **1988**.

IF you are playing a match for an hour and a half on Saturday you shouldn't spend two hours a day training. You don't want to leave all your vitality on the training track.

DANNY BLANCHFLOWER in *The Encyclopedia of Association Football*, **1960**.

ALL the lads have been moaning about him. He dives in yards from the ball and hits you on the legs whether the ball's there or not. No one appreciates that kind of thing, especially in training.

ANONYMOUS BRIGHTON PLAYER on Hans Kraay Jr, Dutch player suspended in Holland but on trial with Brighton, **1983**.

ANOTHER feature of England training is 'mime-practice'. As you jog round, you go through all the motions without a ball that you do when you have the ball. You trap, pass, volley, head for goal, head clear and weight imaginary passes. All that is missing is the ball.

PHIL NEAL, Liverpool and England right-back, in *Attack From The Back*, **1981**.

I have never known a group of people like footballers for eating. A huge evening meal is digested and forgotten by 9.30 pm. Then they still want endless rounds of sandwiches.

ALEC STOCK in *A Little Thing Called Pride*, **1982**.

I saw him on one occasion shift two steak pies, a heaped plate of potatoes and vegetables, two helpings of apple tart and literally gallons of tea.

ROY PAUL, Manchester City and Wales player, of John Charles in *A Red Dragon of Wales*, **1956**.

'A bit crude when eating' states the report of an Arsenal scout. He was referring to a well-known international in whom Arsenal were interested. The description shows how deeply the club vet a man for whose transfer they may make a bid, and the personal background sometimes damns a player who has the necessary football qualifications.

BERNARD JOY in *Forward, Arsenal!*, **1952**.

FOOD may be incidental to some people, but to footballers who have to keep in good physical trim it is extremely important. A Continenal breakfast is not very filling, but requests for a 'decent breakfast' of ham and eggs met with uncomprehending stares.

BILLY LIDDELL, Liverpool and Scotland winger, on trip to Yugoslavia in 1955, in *My Soccer Story*, **1960**.

MY only problem seems to be with Italian breakfasts. No matter how much money you've got, you can't seem to get any Rice Crispies.

LUTHER BLISSETT, just after his transfer from Watford to Milan, **1983**.

THE main thing I miss about London? The sausages.

TERRY VENABLES on life with Barcelona, **1984**.

THE stomach plays a very important part in footer, and lets a chap down badly if it is not in the right condition on the day of the match. In my youth I always had a big meal, an hour or so before the game. That is wrong. The general procedure is a good breakfast and a very light lunch – consisting of boiled mutton, or fish, or – what I consider best – a poached egg on well-crisped toast. If this is carried out faithfully a great improvement will be noticed regarding wind, and you'll find you will be able to last out a hard encounter much easier.

EDDIE HAPGOOD, Arsenal and England full-back, on 'Faults to Avoid in Soccer', in *Boy's Own Paper*, **1939**.

WE have left nothing to chance. The players do not have to swallow a crumb of Russian food is they so wish. We are travelling with a full kitchen of Irish food – rashers, eggs, black pudding, steaks, ketchup. There can be no excuses on this score.

FA OF IRELAND OFFICAL on the Republic's preparations for a match in the Soviet Union, **1985**.

FROM the first time I kicked a ball as a pro nineteen years ago, I began to learn what the game was all about. It's about the drunken parties that go on for days. The orgies, the birds and the fabulous money. Football is just a distraction – but you're so fit you can carry on with all the high living in secret, and still play the game at the highest level.

PETER STOREY, former Arsenal and England player, **1980**.

QUITE a few of them [footballers] can knock back a pint or two, but none are alcoholics.

JIMMY HILL, then Fulham player, in *Striking For Soccer*, **1961**.

WHILE with Spurs I drank heavily to help relieve the pressure of big-time football. My career covered an era when the game suddenly went sick and defeat became a dirty word. We used to get really stoked up for the games, with our adrenalin pumped so high that a lot of us needed an after-match drink to bring us back to earth.

JIMMY GREAVES in *This One's On Me*, **1979**.

FROM what I have seen, the young players of today drink a lot more than during my teenage-to-early-twenties period. We used to be pint sinkers but now the orders are more likely to be Bacardi-and-cokes or gin-and-tonics. I have seen them pay out in a single round what I used to earn in a week at Chelsea.

GREAVES, as above.

I don't drink every day, but when I do it's usually for four or five days on the trot. I've got a drink problem.

GEORGE BEST, **1979**.

I might go to Alcoholics Anonymous, but I think it'd be difficult for me to be anonymous.

BEST, **1980**.

BEST wasn't the first player to be ruined by drink. I see booze as one of the major evils of the game. And its influence has become more widespread now there is big money to be earned. In my day it was half a lager. Today they're drinking spirits.

BOBBY ROBSON in *Time on the Grass*, **1982**.

IT was a different world in hose days. Our big night out was fish and chips and a pint, now it's the Top of the Town or whatever it's called. They take taxis here, chauffeurs even, drink wine, and as for the clothes, well it's a completely changed life today.

PAT WELTON, Spurs youth manager, **1972**.

IF I go into a bar and have a lager shandy, word goes back that I'm knocking back bottles of champagne. By the time it gets to the papers or my manager at Arsenal, it's me lying in the gutter.

CHARLIE NICHOLAS, **1984**.

I won't stand for booze. One player who joined the club said, 'I may as well tell you, I like a drink.' And he did. I found out he was taking others along. You know what it's like – instead of one lager they had three. Three becomes four and it escalates. I had to get rid of him, too.

LOU MACARI, teetotal Swindon manager, **1988**.

I don't have any sort of drink problem, though if it helps to not touch a drop I'll try. But if sex ruined your game, all the married players would be out of a job.

CHARLIE NICHOLAS, **1984**.

OF course a player can have sexual intercourse before a match and play a blinder. But if he did it for six months, he'd be a decrepit old man. It takes the strength from the body.

BILL SHANKLY, **1971**.

WHEN Sam Jones and I arrived at Bloomfield Road in the morning for training, the rest of the lads used to chant: 'They don't drink. They don't smoke. They don't go out with women. What do they live for?' There was a one-word answer to that – football.

PETER DOHERTY, Blackpool, Northern Ireland and a self-confessed fitness freak, on football in the 1930s in *Blackpool Football* by Robin Daniels, **1972**.

ONE bloke admitted he didn't feel right unless he had a bit of sex on Saturday mornings. OK that's fine by me . . . if a player likes a ciggie or two, or a pint at lunchtime or a jump before breakfast that's his business.

TERRY JONES, Tividale manager, in Brian James, *Journey to Wembley*, **1977**.

THERE are a lot of gay footballers who can't talk about their sexuality because most players are so negative about homosexuals.

GERARD van REIJSEN, founder of FC Gay (Amsterdam), **1988**.

I never say I'm going to *play* football. It's work.

MIKE ENGLAND, Spurs and Wales player, in Hunter Davies, *The Glory Game*, **1972**.

I'M sure Sunday-morning players get more pleasure than professionals.

JIMMY PEARCE, Spurs winger, in Hunter Davies, *The Glory Game*, **1972**.

YOU drop your shoulder and move round a defender only to discover he didn't read your first dummy. So you crash straight into him and he comes out with the ball.

TREVOR BROOKING on playing Sunday-morning football for Havering Nalgo, **1985**.

I don't like amateurs. They get up my nose. I know football as my living, as a hard life . . . my wife and child's livelihood. Footballl is a joy to them, plus a tenner in the boot as a bonus. And you can be the local hero in Hitchin or Wycombe. It's nice. No pressure. You have got your job and your family; so you can ponce around every Saturday, do a little bit, and you are a star. Amateurs' lives are a bit luxurious compared to ours.

EAMONN DUNPHY in *Only A Game?*, **1976**.

AMATEURISM and good sportsmanship . . . for this club one is valueless without the other and, if either is surrendered, even in the present difficult world, in the cause of success, the time has surely been reached for the club's life, at least at senior level, to be brought to a close. Euthanasia must come before corruption.

CORINTHIAN-CASUALS centenary brochure, **1983**.

IF you think that Tividale doesn't matter because I've seen the big time you are wrong. At whatever level of football you are talking about everybody wants to play. I'd be as sick at missing the game at Oldbury as I used to be when I looked at the team sheet at St Andrews and saw eleven other names on the list.

DENNIS ISHERWOOD, ex-Birmingham full-back, on playing in the West Midland League for Tividale, in Brian James, *Journey to Wembley*, **1977**.

IT'S not money. The taxman takes half. . . . I sometimes wonder why I give myself two or three hours' driving on top of a day's work just to come here and train. When I get here, I know. It's not for the few quid . . . it's for the football. Knocking a ball about, having a laugh with your mates, getting out of the shower feeling shattered, but alive.

KEN MALLENDER, ex-Sheffield United defender, on playing non-League for Telford, in Brian James, *Journey to Wembley*, 1977.

TIMES were hard for many people. Most of us were brought up to accept discipline, and to discipline ourselves. We didn't have much, so we learned to make the most of what we did have, and if a man was lucky enough to have a job he put everything into it. As a footballer, people looked up to you. No player was going to let that go.

GEORGE MALE, Arsenal and England full-back, on life in the 1930s.

WHEN I first played for my village side I was rewarded with a bag of vegetables and sixpence. At seventeen I was paid £5, and I counted it a dozen times on the way home, thinking I was in the big money. I suppose I was what they call a 'hungry fighter'.

JOE MERCER in *Soccer the British Way*, 1963.

JOHNNY Haynes is a top entertainer and will be paid as one from now on. I will give him £100 a week to play for Fulham.

TOMMY TRINDER, Fulham chairman, after lifting of the maximum wage, 1961.

ITALIAN players wonder how on earth players like Haynes live on such a salary! If anyone suggested that the Italians should play a whole season and bank only £5000, plus another £90 or so in bonuses, there would be a nationwide strike.

JOHN CHARLES, Juventus and Wales, in *The Gentle Giant*, 1962.

I used to take a part-time job away from soccer in summer. We had a supporter who owned a dairy, so a few of us would take jobs as drivers on his milk floats. Other lads would work in the pottery industry around Stoke and Burslem. We had to work or go without.

ROY SPROSON, Port Vale player 1949–71, on life in the lower divisions before the abolition of the maximum wage.

TWENTY pounds a week in the season, and £17 in summer, was no kind of money for men who gave pleasure to millions, and I was the last to blame them for wanting to change things. But the agreement the players won has allowed them to take more money out of the game than it has to give.

ALAN HARDAKER, Football League secretary, on the lifting of the maximum wage in 1961, in *Hardaker of the League*, **1977**.

THIS fear of losing one's job manifested itself when the new contracts were being considered around 1 April each year. At that time of the season all the players, even the stars, were looking into the assistant secretary's office almost every day, asking if there was any news of their contracts. All of them carried an innate fear of not being offered fresh terms for the following season.

BOB WALL, secretary, on Arsenal in the 1930s, in *Arsenal from the Heart*, **1969**.

LAST year I picked up £1200 from Bells. And I've just had a tax bill for £992. I'll fight it . . . but you wonder what's the use of even going to lunch to pick up the prizes when that happens. There was no point my taking a rise [after succeeding Bill Shankly], the tax man would have grabbed it all back.

BOB PAISLEY in Briam James, *Journey to Wembley*, **1977**.

PLAYERS shouldn't need 'extras'. But then you don't see what the tax man does to their wage packets. It's bloody outrageous – they could earn a fortune this year with the treble, and they'll keep about a quarter of it. . . . That's why they turn up at a shop-opening for a hundred quid. Those fees come in readies.

PAISLEY on the players' 'pool' fifteen days before the **1977** FA Cup final, as above.

SOME folks tell me that we professional players are soccer slaves. Well, if this is slavery, give me a life sentence.

BOBBY CHARLTON, **1960**.

ANYBODY who complains about that sort of life wants his head examining.

TONY KAY, Sheffield Wednesday player, on the footballer's lot in **1962**. Three years later Kay received a life ban and prison sentence for his part in a bribes scandal.

To a certain extent football is still like white slavery. We are entertainers, playing to packed galleries every Saturday and often in between. People flock from all four corners of the country to see us perform, to see what it is that makes us stand out from the crowd. But our earnings are unrelated to our crowd-pulling power. . . . It makes me smile when people talk about big-money footballers.

BILLY BREMNER in the programme for his testimonial match which earned him £40,000, **1974**.

THE buying and selling of players sounds rather like a slave market. Moreover the payment of large transfer fees can be the refuge of the incompetent manager.

SIR NORMAN CHESTER, Chairman of committee examining English soccer's problems, **1968**.

I will not be blackmailed into signing for someone I don't want to play for. I am a professional footballer, not a slave.

LEE CHAPMAN on Derby's attempt to prevent his signing for Nottingham Forest by pressuring his French club, Niort, **1988**.

A professional footballer has a duty to his wife and family to earn as much as he can from this sport as quickly as he can.

JOHN WARK on why his £50,000 salary at Ipswich was not enough, **1983**.

THE biggest difference between playing for Forfar and playing for Glasgow Rangers? Probably about two or three hundred pounds a week.

STEWART KENNEDY, former Rangers and Scotland goalkeeper, **1984**.

You can make a player fitter by giving him a pay rise. It might sound daft, but he works harder and he's happier at home.

LOU MACARI, Swindon manager, **1988**.

I don't fine players because at this level, on our wages, hitting them in the wallet only penalizes wives and children and I don't want that on my conscience.

MACARI, **1988**.

I know of no class of work people who are less able to look after themselves than footballers; they are like a lot of sheep. A representative from the union could go and speak to them on why and wherefore they should join, and they would immediately decide to join. Two minutes after, a manager could go and say a few words to them, and they would decide not to join.

CHARLIE ROBERTS in *Football Players' Magazine*, **1914**.

THE worst contract I have ever seen.

LORD WALTER MONCKTON, QC on the Football League forms, **1947**.

I stand here as the representative of the last bonded men in Britain – the professional footballers! We seek your help to smash a system in which human beings are being bought and sold like cattle. A system which, as in feudal times, binds a man to one master or, if he rebels, stops him getting another job. The conditions of the footballer's employment are akin to slavery.

JIMMY GUTHRIE, Chairman of the Association Footballers' and Trainers' Union (forerunner of the Professional Footballers' Association), in speech to TUC at Southport, **1955**.

MANY things are wrong with the British contract system, but the PFA are not militant enough and there is a complete lack of communication among the rank and file. . . . In any other business I could resign from the company and take a job elsewhere. . . . My generation will not put up with it.

DUNCAN MCKENZIE, **1974**.

HE is the Arthur Scargill of football.

ALAN MULLERY, Crystal Palace manager, on PFA secretary Gordon Taylor, **1983**.

LABOUR. Definitely. Aren't all the players Labour?

STEVE PERRYMAN, Spurs player, on his politics, in Hunter Davies, *The Glory Game*, **1972**. Two team-mates shared his views; nine were Tories.

I have never voted anything but Labour in my life. And I never will.

KEVIN KEEGAN, **1980**.

HAVE you noticed how we only win the World Cup under a Labour government?

RT HON HAROLD WILSON MP, Leader of the Opposition, **1971**.

I personally don't hold with those players who say they'd play for England for nothing. So would I in one way. I'd play for Ireland for nothing, if they let everybody in for nothing. If they're collecting a £50,000 gate, playing for hope and glory has nothing to do with the facts.

DANNY BLANCHFLOWER in *The Encyclopedia of Association Football*, **1960**.

I cannot feed my child on glory.

PAOLO ROSSI during pay dispute with Juventus, **1982**.

Two months ago Rossi was over the moon – now he is asking for it.

JUVENTUS official, in response to Italy's World Cup hero, **1982**.

PEOPLE say we do not have the passion to win a World Cup, that it does not mean enough to us. But to me it means everything, the absolute climax of a footballer's career. Club football gives us good rewards. I earn more than £1500 a week with PSV Eindhoven. But the final is above money. This is the end. On Sunday I will give everything.

WILLY VAN DER KERKHOF, Dutch midfield player, before the 1978 World Cup final against Argentina..

AN international player's grandchildren are not going to ask him how much money he earned, but how many caps he won. Playing for your country is an honour, and it is right that this should be recognized by the national association.

ANDY ROXBURGH, Scotland manager, announcing establishment of Scottish Hall of Fame, 1988.

THE failure to understand the physical and mental strains on a professional is behind the widely held belief that footballers are stupid.

JOHAN CRUYFF, Ajax and Holland player, 1973.

WHAT they say about footballers being ignorant is rubbish. I spoke to a couple yesterday and they were quite intelligent.

RAQUEL WELCH, after visit to Chelsea match, 1973.

I prefer players not to be too good or clever at other things. It means they concentrate on football.

BILL NICHOLSON, Spurs manager, 1973.

THE game almost broke the health of a highly intelligent man like Joe Mercer. It cut George Best off at adolescence. It has the power to destroy because it releases unnatural forces. It creates an unreal atmosphere of excitement and it deals in elation and despair and it bestows these emotions at least once a week.

MALCOLM ALLISON in *Colours of My Life*, 1975.

I get on the team bus these days and the back seat is always empty. You used to be in the side for a few years before they'd let you anywhere near the back seat. Now the young lads are all doing *The Times* crossword or playing Scrabble. I'm not saying that's so bad but I find it all a bit hard to take.

ALAN BALL, **1982**.

As a player it's like living in a box. Someone takes you out of the box for training and the games . . . and makes all the decisions for you. I have seen players – famous internationals – in an airport lounge all get up and follow one bloke into the lav. Six of them, maybe, standing there not wanting to piss themselves, but following the bloke who does. Like sheep . . . because that's the way they've been trained: to sit, stand, follow the bloke in front, never asking why. It's daft, but it's the system.

GEOFF HURST, in Brian James, *Journey to Wembley*, **1977**.

FOR the next three years I am not a man, I am not a footballer, I am an industry.

JOHAN CRUYFF on signing for Barcelona, **1973**.

IF I was really unhappy I'd rather go home and play for Flint Town United.

IAN RUSH in Italy, **1988**.

TAKE away Match of the Day and all the hangers-on and it's all very empty and lonely being a footballer.

RODNEY MARSH, **1971**.

THE image of the professional footballer as a glamorous show-business type, surrounded by pretty girls and flash cars, is firmly implanted in most people's minds. I know him more accurately as the deeply insecure family man or the tearful, failed apprentice.

EAMON DUNPHY, **1973**.

WHEN you've been given a free transfer by Rochdale you think seriously about your future.

TERRY DOLAN, Bradford City manager and ex-Rochdale reject, **1987**.

IT's like turtles in the South Sea. Thousands are hatched on the beaches, but few of them reach the water.

STEVE COPPELL, England international and PFA official, on career prospects for young players, **1983**.

IF he doesn't grow up he'll find himself back where he started – on a stall in Shepherd's Bush market.

DAVE BASSETT, Sheffield United manager, on his former Wimbledon midfielder Wally Downes, **1988**.

THE permissive society has given us young footballers totally concerned with what they can get rather than what they ought to be giving.

BERTIE MEE, Arsenal manager, **1974**.

As they wheeled me out of hospital, everybody was looking at me quietly – 'poor chap' – and I didn't want it. I felt, psychologically, as though I needed to do something violent to myself.

STEVE COPPELL on enforced retirement at the age of 27, **1983**.

AT Burnley, no moustaches, no sideburns, long hair discouraged. . . . But when I was at Chelsea I could go through the menu, wine and all, 'phone home for hours, entertain friends, all on the club. If I run up a 2p phone call with Burnley, I get the bill. Keeps your feet on the ground, that, I'm telling you.

COLIN WALDRON, Burnley defender, **1975**.

'I'd teach Bryan Robson not to kick and foul people when things go wrong.'
Brian Clough. *Above left*, Robson reciprocates with his Clough impersonation

'During my six years at Middlesbrough, only goals kept me sane.' Brian Clough.
Above right, portrait of the artist as Boro's angry young man

'I never say I'm going to *play* football. It's work.' Mike England, Spurs
defender, 1972. *Below*, Erik Thorstvedt finds a more relaxed regime at
Tottenham in 1989 as he enjoys the luxury pool

'Football is the opera of the people.' Stafford Heginbotham, Bradford City chairman, 1985. He meant ballet, of course, as performed by Trevor Peake of Coventry and airborne Clive Allen (Spurs)

'In England, soccer is a grey game played by grey people on grey days.' Rodney Marsh in Florida, 1979. Ten years on, there is still gaiety in the old game at Crystal Palace

Right: 'Malcolm had lived a bit in between, and it didn't quite work out.' Peter Swales, Manchester City chairman, on the fedora flash of Allison's career between spells at Maine Road

'Producers started putting pressure on commentators to generate excitement.' *Above left*, Kenneth Wolstenholme, pictured rattling off a nostalgic yarn to Alexei Sayle

'I'm a hero now, but I know I could be a bum in a year's time.' *Above right*, Jack Charlton, reflecting on the short journey from manager to laundry-man

Below right: 'We had our problems with the wee feller, but I prefer to remember his genius.' Sir Matt Busby on George Best, 20 years after shared European Cup glory

'The saddest and most beautiful sight I have ever seen.' Kenny Dalglish on Anfield's Shankly Gates after the Hillsborough tragedy, 1989

IF they [the Albanians] won't let me in, I'll pack my bags and go home. I'm not getting my hair cut for anybody. I'm out there to play football, not to look good. Beards are banned, but I'm not shaving off my stubble either. This is my best and most consistent season, and I've done it unshaven and with this haircut. If the worst comes to the worst, I'll wear a hair net and put a swimming cap on top so they won't see it.

CHRIS WADDLE, Tottenham and England winger, **1989**.

THE only thing I enjoyed during my six years at Middlesbrough was scoring goals. From Saturday to Saturday I was very unhappy. My ability was never utilized, by me or the management. Only goals kept me sane. That was the only pleasure.

BRIAN CLOUGH, **1973**.

I put the ball past the goalkeeper. It's my one regret in all this that the ball didn't finish in the net.

DEREK DOOLEY on the incident which led to his leg being amputated, in Arthur Hopcraft, *The Football Man*, **1968**.

I'M feeling happier. Goals cheer you up..

IAN RUSH after four-goal spree for Juventus, **1987**.

EACH night in bed, I think how I can score a goal – a header, a shot, from a pass . . .

TANJU COLAK, Galatasaray (Turkey) striker and Europe's top scorer in '87–88, **1989**.

5

Philosophers United

PEOPLE get mad over it, people enthuse over it, people exultate and people sadly even have started fighting and destructing over it.

> COLIN MURPHY, Lincoln manager, on football, **1988**.

FOOTBALL is important but life is important too.

> MAXIME BOSSIS of France after semi-final defeat, World Cup, **1986**.

LOOK, there are a lot of other things in life. When I'm at home I don't even think or talk about football. It's not my whole life. I like it, I like playing it, I do not like talking about it.

> RUUD GULLIT, Holland captain, **1988**.

OUTSIDE of family life, there is nothing better than winning European Cups.

> BRIAN CLOUGH, **1980**.

I just happen to be one of those people for whom sport is on the highest possible plane. In a way, I see sport as being something even above real life.

> DAVE SEXTON, Manchester United manager, **1980**.

FOOTBALL'S not a matter of life and death. It's much more important than that.

> BILL SHANKLY, **1960s**.

THERE is more to life than cricket.

IAN BOTHAM on turning out for Scunthorpe reserves, **1980**.

AT the end of the day it's not the end of the world.

JIM MCLEAN, Dundee United manager, after UEFA Cup final defeat, **1987**.

BEING given chances and not taking them – that's what life is all about.

RON GREENWOOD, England manager, **1982**.

THE missing of chances is one of the mysteries of life.

SIR ALF RAMSEY, **1972**.

REPORTER: It was a funny game, Jim.
JIMMY SIRREL: Human beings are funny people.

EXCHANGE after Arsenal *v* Notts County match, **1982**.

WE held them for 89 minutes, then they kippered us.

DOGAN ARIF, Fisher Athletic manager, on losing to Telford, **1987**.

WHEN their second goal went in, I knew our pig was dead.

DANNY WILLIAMS, Swindon manager, after FA Cup defeat by West Ham, **1975**.

TRUE, after the game the players felt they had been kicked in the teeth by the result, but then we have big teeth and we will come straight back.

JOHN HOLLINS, shortly before his demise as Chelsea manager, **1988**.

I just wish I could go out to the supermarket and buy 11 pairs of fresh legs for the replay.

FRANK CONNOR, Raith Rovers manager, after drawing with Rangers in Scottish Cup, **1988**.

IT was like the Alamo out there. We had one shot, but we shot the chief.

EDDIE MCCLUSKEY, Enfield manager, on FA Cup victory at Leyton Orient, **1988**.

A third-round replay would be a cup run for us.

JOE ROYLE, Oldham manager, before FA Cup tie *v* Tottenham, **1988**.

THEY all seemed to have longer legs than my players. When they came forward it was like the Charge of the Light Brigade.

BRIAN HALL, Yeovil manager, on First Division QPR's FA Cup win, **1988**.

OBVIOUSLY for Scunthorpe it would be a nice scalp to put Wimbledon on their bottoms.

DAVE BASSETT, Wimbledon manager, **1984**.

AND they were lucky to get nil.

LEN SHACKLETON after his six-goal debut for Newcastle in 13–0 defeat of Newport, **1946**.

I'VE heard of players selling dummies, but this club keeps buying them.

SHACKLETON on Newcastle United, **1970s**.

How could I avoid being Player of the Year playing behind our defence?

PAT JENNINGS, then of Spurs, accepting Footballer of the Year award, **1973**.

PEOPLE keep on about stars and flair. As far as I'm concerned you find stars in the sky and 'flair' is something on the bottom of trousers.

GORDON LEE, Everton and Newcastle manager, **1970s**.

THERE is a rat in the camp trying to throw a spanner in the works.

CHRIS CATTLIN, Brighton manager, **1983**.

I'M one of the best full-backs in the country. Trouble is, we play in a lot of towns . . .

TERRY NAYLOR, Tottenham defender, **1978**.

NEVER in the history of the FAI Cup had a team wearing hooped jerseys lost a final in a year ending in 5.

HOME FARM FC (Dublin) programme notes, **1985**.

CLAIM to fame outside soccer: I once put together an MFI wardrobe in less than four days.

TERRY GIBSON, Coventry striker, **1985**.

I have other irons in the fire, but I'm keeping them close to my chest.

JOHN BOND, on leaving Manchester City manager's job, **1983**.

EVEN when you're dead, you shouldn't let yourself lie down and be buried.

GORDON LEE, after losing Everton manager's job, **1981**.

WE'RE halfway round the Grand National course with many hurdles to clear. So let's make sure we all keep our feet firmly on the ground.

MIKE BAILEY, Charlton manager, on his team's promotion chances, **1981**.

WE'RE like Lady Di. She's not the Queen yet. She's not even married. But like us, she's nicely placed.

JIMMY SIRREL, Notts County manager, on his side's promotion prospects, **1981**.

MY ambition is to meet Prince Charles. I call him 'King'.

ALAN BALL, **1979**.

WHEN you come to a place like Barcelona you think, 'Bloody hell, I wish I was back in England.'

TERRY BUTCHER, Ipswich defender, 1979.

SEE one wall, you've seen them all.

JOHN TREWICK, West Bromwich midfielder, at the Great Wall of China, 1978.

I don't even know where Albania is yet, but I'll be finding out shortly.

STEVE BULL, Wolves striker, on England Under-21 call-up, 1989.

IT's like going to a different country.

IAN RUSH on life in Italy, 1988.

IF we lose to Italy, we might as well pack our bags and go home.

FRANZ BECKENBAUER, West German manager, at European Championships . . . in West Germany, 1988.

AFRICA? We're not in bloody Africa, are we?

GORDON LEE, Everton manager, asked his impressions of Africa during tour of Morocco, 1978.

IF the African nations ever succeeded in their plan for one British team in the World Cup, I'd vote Tory. I ask you, a load of spear-throwers trying to dictate our role in world football.

BRIAN CLOUGH, 1987.

SOME of the opponents are afraid to tackle me too hard, but I have told them there is nothing to worry about. When I score, I want to feel I've got a genuine goal.

PRESIDENT DOE of Liberia, army master-sergeant turned politician, on his keenness for football, 1988.

OUR interpreter was on his usual hobby-horse, telling a few of the lads of the tremendous good Russia was doing in the world today, when in typical down-to-earth Lancashire fashion, my room-mate Tommy Banks (Bolton Wanderers) interrupted with, 'Ay, that's all very well, but what about Hungary!'

TOM FINNEY in *Finney on Football*, **1958**.

Now that the brief visit of the Dynamo team has come to an end it is possible to say publicly what many people were saying privately before the Dynamos ever arrived. That is, that sport is an unfailing cause of ill-will, and that if such a visit as this had any effect at all on Anglo-Soviet relations, it could only be to make them worse than before.

GEORGE ORWELL in *Tribune*, **1945**.

EVEN if George Orwell's Big Brother is ruling us in 1984, people will still be talking about football.

NEIL FRANKLIN, Stoke and England centre-half, in *Soccer at Home and Abroad*, **1956**.

SOCCER is the biggest thing that's happened in creation, bigger than any 'ism' you can name.

ALAN BROWN, Sunderland manager, **1968**.

I'M a people's man, a player's man. You could call me a humanist.

BILL SHANKLY, **1970**.

WHAT wonderful goals. You really ought to take a closer look at them.

SIR NEVILLE HENDERSON, British Ambassador in Berlin, offering his binoculars to Goering during England's 6–3 win *v* Germany, **1938**

GOD's judgement, which according to classic myths is part of every
battle between two peoples, willed that luck fell on the German side
in the game.

CHANCELLOR HELMUT SCHMIDT in telegram to President Mitterrand after West
Germany's penalties' win in World Cup semi-final *v* France, **1982**.

I know more about football than politics.

RT HON. HAROLD WILSON MP, **1974**.

THE politics involved make me nostalgic for the Middle East.

DR HENRY KISSINGER after FIFA rejected his USA bid to stage 1986 World Cup.

THERE'S a hell of a lot of politics in football. I don't think Henry
Kissinger would have lasted forty-eight hours at Old Trafford.

TOMMY DOCHERTY, **1982**.

I thought the No. 10, Whymark, played exceptionally well.

RT HON. MRS MARGARET THATCHER MP, at the FA Cup final, **1978**. Whymark, listed in
the programme, did not play.

CRICKET shouldn't be used as a political football.

DAVID GRAVENEY, Gloucestershire captain, **1986**.

FOOTBALL is the opera of the people.

STAFFORD HEGINBOTHAM, Bradford City chairman, **1985**.

LEAGUE football is a rat-race of the first magnitude.

BOB LORD, Burnley chairman, **1968**.

IT'S a rat-race – and the rats are winning.

TOMMY DOCHERTY, **1982**.

WHEN one door opens, another smashes you in the face.

DOCHERTY on his dismissal by Preston, **1981**.

PRESTON? They're one of my old clubs. But then most of them are. I've had more clubs than Jack Nicklaus.

DOCHERTY, **1979**.

I'VE been in more courts than Bjorn Borg.

DOCHERTY, **1981**.

CANON League? Some teams are so negative they could be sponsored by Kodak.

DOCHERTY on his return from Australia, **1983**.

I talk a lot. On any subject. Which is always football.

DOCHERTY, **1967**.

YOU know you're getting on when they knock down the ground where you made your debut.

PAT JENNINGS on the bulldozing of White City Stadium, where he first played for Watford against QPR in 1963, **1986**.

PEOPLE keep on about Total Football, but all I know about is Total Petrol.

DEREK DOUGAN, Wolves and Northern Ireland striker, **1973**.

IT's ridiculous, I've served more time than Ronnie Biggs did for the Great Train Robbery.

MALCOLM ALLISON, Plymouth manager, appealing against touchline ban, **1978**.

IT's a cross I'll have to bear. Unlike when I was playing – I couldn't bear crosses then.

DAI DAVIES, ex-Everton and Wales goalkeeper, on having to take time off from his bookshop to play for Bangor City in Europe, **1985**.

IT is our new tactics. We equalize before the others have scored.

DANNY BLANCHFLOWER, **1958**.

A penalty is a cowardly way to score.

PELE, **1966**. His thousandth goal came from the spot.

I go much faster
Than those who run
Without thinking

PELE, *My Life and the Beautiful Game*, **1977**.

IT's my own fault for scoring such marvellous goals. Since I score so many people get used to them and it doesn't seem so important.

HUGO SANCHEZ, Real Madrid striker, explaining fans' lack of appreciation of him, **1988**.

IT's like the difference between a soldier walking through Aldershot and one walking through Belfast. There's a state of mind necessary for the latter if you're to survive.

HOWARD WILKINSON, Sheffield Wednesday manager, on difference between First and Second Divisions, **1984**.

PREPARING the side is just like the matador dressing up to go in the ring. The adrenalin is flowing and he feels ready. The only problem is he has to face the bull. We will have to face the bull next season, and I don't intend to go jumping behind any barriers.

DANNY BERGARA, Uruguayan-born ex-Seville player, on his hopes as manager of . . . Rochdale, **1988**.

EACH season is like a woman having a baby. Winning the Cup was a nice baby. At the moment our baby is the stand. It is a bit of a jumbo and there is a hell of a problem with delivery.

DAVE SEXTON, Chelsea manager, on the club's multi-million-pound West Stand, **1973**.

IN terms of a fifteen-round boxing match we're not getting past the first round. The tempo is quicker. Teams will pinch your dinner from under your noses. They don't give you a chance to play. If you don't heed the warnings, you get nailed to the cross.

GORDON MILNE, Leicester manager, on his team's adjustment to the First Division and after heavy home defeat, **1983**.

I feel like jumping over the moon.

ALF RAMSEY, after Ipswich's League championship success in **1962** – an early case of soccer moon-leaping.

I am not one to jump over the moon or off a cliff.

SIR ALF RAMSEY, **1973**.

I read in the newspapers that Terry Neill says he'll put the joy back in Tottenham's football. What's he going to do – give them bloody banjos?

EDDIE BAILY, ex-assistant manager of Spurs, **1974**.

THE trouble that day was that they used an orange-coloured ball. Eric Caldow and I [the full-backs] were afraid to kick it and Billy McNeill [of Celtic] was afraid to touch it.

BOBBY SHEARER, Rangers defender, on Scotland's 9–3 defeat by England, **1961**.

ALL visiting teams complain about the pitch – but they all seem to win.

ARCHBISHOP MAKARIOS to Dunfermline players visiting Cyprus for a European tie, **1968**. The Scots won 2–0. In Paterson and Scott, *Black and White Magic*.

OF course I'm against Sunday soccer. It'll spoil my Saturday nights.

JOHN RITCHIE, Stoke centre-forward, **1974**.

AFTER all, I could have a drink on a Saturday night without worrying about running around the next morning.

DAVE BEASANT, Newcastle's £850,000 goalkeeper, recalling his conversion from outfield in Sunday park football, **1988**.

HE thought he was playing 4–2–4 in a five-a-side match.

SPEAKER at Liverpool Ramblers FC dinner, **1967**.

ALL-out attack mixed with caution.

JIM MCLAUGHLIN, Shamrock Rovers manager, on his tactics for European tie, **1985**.

IT was a great game – there were goalmouth incidents all over the field.

BURTON ALBION player after FA Trophy tie *v* Kidderminster, **1989**.

HIS problem was that they kept passing the ball to his wrong feet.

LEN SHACKLETON on an unidentified player.

I hope you both lose.

BILL SHANKLY to Joe Mercer before Derby County *v* Manchester City, **1972**, when Liverpool, Derby, Leeds and City were chasing the championship.

IT only takes a second to score a goal.

BRIAN CLOUGH, **1984**.

IF ye dinnae score, ye dinnae win.

JIMMY SIRREL, Notts County manager, **1983**.

THE best team always wins. The rest is only gossip.

SIRREL, **1985**.

FISHING and nature, especially birds, I have loved, although the one passion of my life has been football – the most exhilarating game I know, and the strongest protest against selfishness, without sermonizing, that was ever put before a thoughtful people.

JOHN GOODALL, Preston, Derby and England player, 1889–98, in Andrew Ward and Anton Rippon, *The Derby County Story*, **1983**.

ALL that I know most surely about morality and the obligations of man, I owe to football.

ALBERT CAMUS, **1957**. Camus, French philosopher-novelist, kept goal for Oran FC in Algeria.

I happen to believe that no one can work miracles and it strikes me that applies even to people like Holmes and Watson, the Marx Brothers, Bilko, Inspector Clouseau or Winston Churchill. All these had immeasurable qualities but I don't know whether any of them had the attributes to be able to win promotion for Lincoln City FC with all the injuries and suspensions we have had.

COLIN MURPHY, Lincoln manager, from his programme column 'Murph's Message', **1988**.

AFTER today's match we have the Nottingham Forest game on Sunday to look forward to when, after, which you can all take a well earned rest and maybe whistle a few balls around a few ear holes.

MURPHY, as above, after Lincoln had secured promotion from the GM Vauxhall Conference, **1988**.

HOWEVER we are now into a new season and I have no doubt that George and Mildred are delighted to be selling their cheese rolls in the Fourth Division. . . . So let's look forward to the season and if we all remember that the fires of war should have some good feelings then we shall not be far short at the finish.

MURPHY, as above, on Lincoln's return to the League, **1988**.

METAL fatigue. That is wind, rain, hail and snow and at times the
four seasons in one. The turbulent ride which investigates and
stresses the defects. Not the aircraft in flight but the managerial
role. . . . Incidentally, in conclusion, the metal does not have brain
power.

MURPHY, as above, **1988**.

IT is important to consider that the season is in my view a 'campaign'
and therefore the times for such judgements need to be after 46
matches when after the cannibals have mixed the ingredients in the
boiling pot then, and quite correctly in my view, we shall be eaten
alive, held on simmer or as was the case last year, obtain some
tremendous taste from having formulated the correct recipe.

MURPHY, as above, **1988**.

MUSIC soothes the savage breast. The cobra has been tamed.
Losing. A losing sequence, namely three games, always appears to
put doubts in people's minds irrespective of the club's predicament
and the doubting Thomas's doubt no more and the judges become
experts. The cobra has an excellent habit of wriggling free and
indeed Gordon Hobson wriggled three at Burnley.

MURPHY, as above, **1988**.

I quite often think in programme notes there is a great deal of clap
trap where subconsciously people tend to become excuse worthy. I
have often said to the players that there is talking and doing. Today
will be a day of doing. At least we know the macabre has a habit of
flourishing in different settings.

MURPHY, as above, **1989**.

6

Thoughts of Chairmen Now

THIS page has been left blank in accordance with the author's wishes.

PUBLISHER'S FOOTNOTE to chapter heading. 'The Average Director's Knowledge of Football', in Len Shackleton's *Clown Prince of Soccer*, **1955**.

I gave up football the day I went back to Maine Road and saw the chairman signing autographs.

MIKE SUMMERBEE, former Manchester City winger, **1988**.

As a group (club directors) are totally unrepresentative of football supporters – all white, all male, almost all over 50.

DAVID HELLIWELL, Halifax councillor and Town fan, **1987**.

FOOTBALL chairmen are almost to a man butchers and sausage-meat manufacturers, pork-pie impresarios, industrial and property moguls.

DAVID TRIESMAN, sociologist-journalist, in *Seven Days*, **1973**.

I flew to Paris for the Real Madrid final with the Liverpool directors, and a more disagreeable bunch of people I've rarely encountered. I'd sooner take my chances with a bunch of so-called hooligans. They talked about players as if they were below-stairs staff. Their attitude towards them was so patronizing it was almost Victorian.

JOHN PEEL, disc-jockey and Liverpool fan in *When Saturday Comes*, **1987**.

WHILE I was in the car park the directors all trooped out to join the coach and they walked past me without a single word of greeting. I never even got a good morning from one of them. It was as though I didn't exist. If somebody had stuck a knife in me at that moment, it couldn't have hurt me more.

PAT JENNINGS, Spurs goalkeeper, on learning that the club did not want him any more, **1977**.

WHEN I was a player, if a director spoke to you it was a red-letter day. Now at some clubs you even have players drinking with directors, a crazy situation which puts more pressure on the manager.

BOBBY COLLINS, former Leeds and Scotland captain, **1988**.

FOOTBALL hooligans? Well there are the ninety-two club chairmen for a start.

BRIAN CLOUGH, **1980**.

I have never been so insulted by anyone in football as this little upstart puppy.

DENIS HILL-WOOD Arsenal chairman, announcing that he had written to FA asking them to charge Clough with bringing the game into disrepute, **1980**.

I am struck by the parallels between the disorder which characterizes the approach of some football boardrooms and the disorderly behaviour of the minority of the game's followers.

NEIL MACFARLANE MP, Minister for Sport, **1983**.

FOOTBALL directors are nobody's friends except when there are Cup Final tickets to give away.

ROY HATTERSLEY MP in *Goodbye to Yorkshire*, **1976**.

THE ideal board of directors should be made up of three men – two dead and the other dying.

TOMMY DOCHERTY, **1977**.

You could put his knowledge of the game on a postage stamp. He wanted us to sign Salford Van Hire because he thought he was a Dutch international.

FRED EYRE, former assistant manager at Wigan, on a powerful director, **1981**.

WHEN I came to Manchester as a 15-year-old from the North East, I didn't know what a director was or what he did. My dad would have explained it as someone who didn't work.

BOBBY CHARLTON on becoming a Manchester United director, **1985**.

ONLY women and horses work for nothing.

DOUG ELLIS, Aston Villa's first paid director, **1983**.

A man who gives himself up to football, body and soul . . . will take risks and get himself entangled in such a way as he would never dream of in the conduct of his own business.

SIR FREDERICK WALL, FA secretary, in *Fifty Years of Football*, **1935**.

WHEN I was a director of Sheffield United for six months, the chairman told me normal business standards didn't apply in football. It was the most stupid advice I ever had.

MIKE WATTERSON, Derby chairman, **1982**.

I hold that players are the club's best assets. If that is so, they must be dealt with grandly. We are not looking for a bargain, but for the great players, and he deserves everything that his rank and artistry can get.

DON RAIMUNDO SAPORTA, vice-president of Real Madrid, **1961**.

FOOTBALL is like running a shop. You need first-class products and attractive premises. It's no good having a nice shop if you don't have the right stuff on display.

ERIC SAWYER, 1960s' Liverpool director who persuaded fellow directors to give Bill Shankly unprecedented freedom to build the modern Liverpool FC. Recounted by chief executive Peter Robinson, **1988**.

THE people who come to watch us play, who love the team and regard it as part of their lives, would never appreciate Liverpool having a huge balance in the bank. They want every asset we possess to be wearing a red shirt, and that's what I want, too.

KENNY DALGLISH, **1988**.

IF a chairman is to be held responsible for playing success or failure or indeed monotonous competence, I am prepared to stand up and be counted.

JIMMY HILL, after resigning as Coventry chairman, **1983**.

THE club is running smoothly on the right lines. We are looking forward to consolidating Coventry City in the First Division of the Football League.

JOHN POYNTON, Coventry chairman, at start of club's *22nd* successive season in the First Division, **1988**.

ONE wonders today, however, what some businesses would be like if they were run on the same haphazard lines as most football clubs still are. The amateur director has been kicked out of most industrial and commercial boardrooms. But not in football.

DEREK DOUGAN, Wolves striker, in *Football as a Profession*, co-authored with Percy M. Young, **1974**.

THIS is your club now. I love you all. I am going to come amongst you this afternoon.

DOUGAN, then Wolves' chief executive, addressing crowd before first game after escape from liquidation, **1982**.

THERE's nobody else the supporters can blame if you think about it. They can't blame Malcolm Allison cos he's not here; they can't blame John Bond cos he isn't here; they can't blame Billy McNeill cos he isn't here. Jim (Frizzell) has only been here since Christmas. So I'm the only one, aren't I?

PETER SWALES, Manchester City chairman, **1987**.

PETER Swales? He works hard. Likes publicity, though. He wears a card round his neck saying, 'In case of heart attack call a press conference.'

TOMMY DOCHERTY, **1982**.

SACKING a manager is as big an event in my life as drinking a glass of beer. I'd hire 20 managers a year if I wanted to – 100 if necessary.

JESUS GIL, President of Atletico Madrid, **1989**.

THE chairman should never say, 'If we don't win the League, the manager's out.' You have to judge things like that at the end of the season.

MARTIN EDWARDS, Manchester United chairman, in the pre-season period 10 weeks before sacking Ron Atkinson, **1986**.

SACKING the manager is not the answer to Fulham's or indeed football's problems. What went on at Manchester City and Palace recently is disgusting. So, for that matter, were the events at Norwich. Contracts should be honoured both ways.

ERNIE CLAY, Fulham chairman, two days before he dismissed manager Bobby Campbell, **1980**.

I don't feel under any pressure from the chairman. He has been great, like a father to me. People are saying I am living in the shadow of the sack. All I can say is that the chairman has told me I've got a contract with him for life.

BOBBY CAMPBELL shortly before he was sacked by Clay, **1980**.

WE'RE backing the best boss in the business. Billy Bremner is under contract for two more years and will be staying at this club as manager. Reports and rumours to the contrary have been deeply upsetting and plainly untrue. We have no intention of replacing him.

LESLIE SILVER, Leeds chairman, a month before Bremner was fired, **1988**.

I remember the late Alan Ball senior telling me what his chairman said to him when he was appointed manager of Preston. Posing for a photographer, the chairman put his arm round Alan and said, 'We sink or swim together.' Two years later, Alan was called in to see the board and knew in advance that they were going to sack him. He asked, 'How many of you are going to sink with me?' Of course none of them did.

BOBBY ROBSON in *Time on the Grass*, **1982**.

THE man who sacked me [at Fulham] was Eric Miller – you know, Sir Eric Miller, the property developer who shot himself. Shows how he reacted to pressure doesn't it?

BOBBY ROBSON, **1981**.

I'VE sacked him [Brian Clough] on three occasions in the last two years, and told him to bugger off out of the club.

SAM LONGSON, Derby County chairman, **1973**.

EVEN I could manage this lot.

LONGSON after Clough's departure, **1973**.

I could understand why Brian [Clough] hardly ever went to board meetings at Derby, because while I was there I found it difficult to get any sense out of them. There was one director who used to snoop about the dressing-rooms and kitchens. He'd go into the kitchen and say to the woman in charge, 'I see you've got an extra bottle of brandy – where did you get that from?' It was like having a spy walking around.

TOMMY DOCHERTY in *Call The Doc*, **1981**.

THE Villa chairman, Doug Ellis, said he was right behind me. I told him I'd sooner have him in front of me where I could see him.

TOMMY DOCHERTY, **1970**.

YOUR mouth is obviously bigger than mine. I suggest you run your club in your way and leave us to run ours.

ARTHUR WAIT, Crystal Palace chairman, in letter to Bob Lord, Burnley chairman, who had criticized Palace's high bonuses, **1970**.

YOU have to be crackers to be a director of a football club. Who'd pour money into football when you can earn 10 or 20 per cent with it?

ARTHUR WAIT, **1971**.

IF you thought Bob Lord was rude, you've heard nothing yet.

JOHN JACKSON, Burnley chairman, after row over tickets at Chelsea, **1982**.

IF everything I hear about Ken Bates is true, I can't understand why he doesn't push Johnny Hollins to one side and manage the club himself. Bates is one of those stubborn, opinionated, know-all types who thinks he can do everything. And probably can!

JIMMY GREAVES, **1988**.

I'M off to my 300-acre farm. You lot can bugger off to your council houses.

KEN BATES, Chelsea chairman, to the press after club's relegation, **1988**.

MY chairman Robert Maxwell, they ought to let him run football.

JIM SMITH, Oxford United manager, **1983**.

MAXWELL has the posture and manners of the dominant male.

DR DESMOND MORRIS, author of *The Naked Ape* and a co-director of Maxwell's at Oxford, **1983**.

I understand and sympathize with their strong feelings, but I cannot accept their conservatism or parochialism.

ROBERT MAXWELL on reaction of Oxford and Reading fans to proposed merger as Thames Valley Royals, **1983**.

HE stole the glory from the players and spoiled a night that should have been for the players and supporters.

JIM SMITH, Oxford manager, on how Maxwell attacked the local council at the club's promotion celebrations, **1985**.

I have played football since I was a toddler. Left wing, as you would expect. I was very fast.

MAXWELL, **1985**.

THE chairman said at the start of the season that we would compete with the big clubs. We have fulfilled out fixtures, but we have not competed in the manner meant at the time.

ARTHUR COX, Derby manager, on Maxwell's failure to allow him to buy players during Derby's first season back in the First Division, **1987–88**.

MR Maxwell is one of the few men who is in a position to stop the drain of British football talent to the Continent. If he bought only one or two of Rush, Lineker, Hateley, Hoddle or Hughes for Derby, that would be far more beneficial than a coach who, although a great player, has yet to prove himself in management.

COX on Maxwell's offer of a job as 'technical director' to Johan Cruyff, **1988**.

THERE are still some things that baffle me about the bloke [Maxwell]. Like why he loves seeing his mug across the back pages, because Robert Redford he ain't.

BRIAN CLOUGH, **1987**.

MAXWELL'S just bought Brighton and Hove Albion, and he's furious to find that it's only one club.

TOMMY DOCHERTY, **1988**.

I might very well be able to talk a top manager like Brian Clough into coming to Boro, but what good would that do? I'd probably only get myself a bloke who wanted to keep me out of the way.

ALF DUFFIELD, Middlesbrough chairman, explaining his decision to appoint Willie Maddren as manager in **1985**. Eighteen months later Middlesbrough were relegated and Duffield resigned, having already sacked Maddren.

AT other clubs the directors probably get worried if things aren't going well, and they don't like to have people coming up to them criticizing in pubs and at parties. Well, that doesn't influence me at all. If people start telling me what's wrong with the team I just say, 'Look, why don't you f – awff.'

PATRICK COBBOLD, Ipswich chairman, **1981**.

I'VE heard claims that I'm supposed to be using Mafia money. Some football clubs are in such a mess right now you could buy them out of Brownie funds.

ANTON JOHNSON, then Rotherham chairman, on his part in club takeovers, **1983**.

I pay their wages and so that gives me the right to pick the team.

HERBERT METCALFE, Bradford Park Avenue chairman, six months before the League voted the club out, **1969**.

OUR long-term aim is to get back in the League. We may have to start in the West Riding County Amateur League. It won't be a six-month thing – we want to make nice, steady progress. At the moment we have no ground, no manager and no team.

BOB ROBINSON, chairman-elect of re-formed Park Avenue, **1988**.

I missed the last goal. I was too busy counting our share of the money.

KEN BATES, Chelsea chairman, after Full Members final had produced receipts of £508,000, **1986**.

THE only way they [Nottingham Forest players] will get European bonuses is if the club's directors have a whip-round. But I've never seen pigs fly.

BRIAN CLOUGH, **1983**.

WE have no desire just to be a football club. That is not the basis of success.

PAUL BOBROFF, chairman of Tottenham Hotspur plc, **1983**.

THERE used to be a football club over there.

KEITH BURKINSHAW, former Spurs manager, as he left Tottenham Hotspur plc for the last time, **1984**.

THE club have made it clear that fans should be grateful that the lower tier of terracing on the East Stand is being maintained . . . though it's likely that it will soon go, to be replaced by a wine bar or a short-haul runway for the box-holders' private aircraft.

OFF THE BALL magazine on Spurs' demolishing The Shelf terrace, **1988**.

IRVING Scholar's [Spurs chairman] aggressive stance towards football as a business is offset by the typically cavalier dismissal of his customers. As an organization which offers insurance against late cancellation, we would be unlikely to get a deal from any company if more of the game's administrators showed his attitude.

MONICA HARTLAND, deputy chairman National Federation of Football Supporters Clubs, after Spurs cancelled the opening match of the season on the morning of the game because the ground was not ready, **1988**.

YOU can't put a price on the value of clearing our name, but at that price we'd like to buy two points every week.

IRVING SCHOLAR after Spurs had won back two points deducted and been fined instead, **1988**.

WE don't recognize *any* supporters' associations. I don't mind them existing – just won't have anything to do with them. I never go to Supporters' Dinners; it only costs a fiver or so to go, but then they think they own you. In particular, I never accept money from supporters' associations; they hand you a couple of cheques for a few thousand, and the next thing you know they're demanding a seat on the Board in return . . . My ambition, what we are aiming for, is for the club to function completely without any money coming through the turnstiles at all. That is the road to Utopia.

BOB LORD, Burnley chairman, **1973**.

JOHN Hall is trying to come in here and purloin the family silver.

GORDON MCKEAG, Newcastle chairman, on Hall's Magpie Group takeover bid, **1988**.

THE fans should ask McKeag who paid for the family silver in the first place. By rights it belongs to them.

JOHN HALL, millionaire property developer and leader of the Magpie Group, **1988**.

I could have doubled my money had I accepted one particular bid for my shares, but I have decided the only items on sale here now are sponsorship, pies and Bovril.

ANGUS COOK, Dundee chairman, **1988**.

I'VE always fancied owning a football team. I might have preferred Chelsea but as they're not for sale, Watford would be a good bet. They are a good family club.

PAUL RAYMOND, Soho nightlife connoisseur, when Elton John put Watford up for sale, **1988**.

THERE won't be any topless teams.

RAYMOND, **1988**.

WATFORD is not Soho, and probably never will be.

IAN RIDLEY, the *Guardian*, on Raymond's attempt to buy Watford, **1988**.

EVERYONE on the Board wants to return to The Valley as much as the fans do. But what can we do if we haven't got the money? There is a pitch available on Blackheath Common – we can't just go up and build a stadium around it.

DEREK UFTON, Charlton director, **1988**.

STRANGE how a ground can catch hold of you. I came past The Valley tonight and found myself staring at it. All those memories! We had to go back didn't we?

ROGER ALWEN, Charlton chairman, announcing return 'home', **1989**.

How can a club that once had John Aldridge and Tommy Tynan on its books get in this position? What has been going on? I come in and all I get is winding-up threats. Sometimes the crises around Newport boggle my mind.

JERRY SHERMAN, American chairman of Newport County, as they faced extinction, **1989**.

IT would be like giving more drink to an alcoholic.

BARRY BATEY, Sunderland director, on plan to raise more money to give to Lawrie McMenemy for team-strengthening, **1987**.

WE'VE got a long-term plan for this club and apart from the results it's going well.

ERNIE CLAY, Fulham chairman, **1980**.

MY apologies to all of you for supporting us through this trying season.

VINCE BARKER, Hartlepool United chairman, in final programme of **1983–84**.

OF course we're going to continue competing in Europe. How else can we get our duty-free cigarettes?

JOHN COBBOLD, Ipswich chairman, **1973**.

YOU ask what constitutes a crisis here. Well, if we ran out of white wine in the boardroom.

PATRICK COBBOLD, Ipswich chairman, **1982**.

IT wasn't so much the death threats or the vandalism, but when you sit with your family in the directors' box and hear a couple of thousand people chanting 'Gilbert Blades is a wanker', then you feel it's time to go.

GILBERT BLADES, ex-Lincoln City chairman, on his resignation, in Anton Rippon, *Soccer: the Road to Crisis*, **1983**.

FOOTBALLERS couldn't run a fish and chip shop.

BOB LORD, Burnley chairman and butcher, **1961**.

WE want to clean up the game, yet the chairmen seem to be motivated purely by self-preservation. At one time one of them said, 'Why blame it on the club when the players are responsible?'

GORDON TAYLOR, players' union secretary, after League chairmen voted down proposal to deduct points from clubs with bad disciplinary records, **1988**.

I can see nice things in the game – when a winger makes a good cross, for instance – but I usually fail to know who has scored the goals. I am a tennis player and a skier.

SAM HAMMAM, Lebanese-businessman and Wimbledon's owner, **1988**.

I'M drinking from a cup today. I'd like a mug, but they're all in the Boardroom.

TOMMY DOCHERTY, **1988**.

7

Ladies in Waiting

MOST Dangerous Opponent: My ex-wife.

> FRANK WORTHINGTON, in answer to magazine questionnaire, **1982**.

MY wife says it would be better if there was another woman. At least then she'd know what she was up against. But she says, 'How can I compete with a football?'

> DON MACKAY, Blackburn Rovers manager, **1988**.

How's the wife?

> TOMMY DOCHERTY to Altrincham physio, 69-year-old Jeff Warburton, **1987**.

A bad wife, of course, can ruin a player's career . . . just as she would ruin any man's career! A good wife is a blessing from above, constituting, as she does, the perfect sheet-anchor for a young athlete to tie himself to.

> TOM FINNEY, Preston and England forward, in *Finney on Football*, **1958**.

YOU can have no idea what it's like in the League. Every big game and there they all sit in a group . . . the wives. The bitchiness and backbiting that go on would turn your stomach. You'd think it was Miss World. You should hear them when things are going wrong. Every girl can only see her own man's skill . . . and the faults in all the others.

> JUDITH HURST, wife of Geoff, in Brian James, *Journey to Wembley*, **1977**.

BETTER to marry an over-priced star than a free transfer I always say.

JUDITH HURST quoting bitchy banter among wives as above.

ISN'T one of the main features of football-match attendance still that it enables men to get away from nagging wives?

FRANK BURROWS, Portsmouth manager, **1981**.

I was conscious of a red-headed woman with her husband leaning over the fence to my right. She shrieked at me: 'Not that way, *that* way!' It's bad enough to be told what to do on the field by men without having women butting in; so on the spur of the moment I turned and said to her: 'Don't hen-peck me, hen-peck him!'

JIMMY HILL in *Striking for Soccer*, **1961**.

WE hope to revive the old tradition of the husband going to football on Christmas day, while the wives cook the turkey.

ERIC WHITE, Brentford official, **1983**.

MY idea of relaxation: Going somewhere away from the wife.

TERRY FENWICK, QPR captain, in *Match* magazine, **1986**.

JOHN Bond has blackened my name with his insinuations about the private lives of football managers. Both my wives are upset.

MALCOLM ALLISON, **1983**.

MY wife has been magic about it.

JOHN BOND, when the story of his affair with a Manchester City employee broke two days after his resignation as manager, **1983**.

BASICALLY, he [Bill Nicholson] doesn't think women have any place in football. I never saw him play for Spurs and I'm not allowed to go and see them now. I feel an outsider really, as if I was a member of the opposition.

GRACE NICHOLSON, wife of then Spurs manager, in Hunter Davies, *The Glory Game*, **1972**.

OF course I didn't take my wife to see Rochdale as an anniversary present. It was her birthday. Would I have got married during the football season? And anyway it wasn't Rochdale, it was Rochdale Reserves.

BILL SHANKLY.

WHEN I lose I've got to talk about it. Some keep it inside them. I go home and relive it with the wife. She just nods and says yes or no.

NORMAN HUNTER, Leeds and England defender, **1973**.

I used to stand up and glare around when fans were giving Geoff stick and they all used to shout: 'Wasn't me, Mrs Hurstie . . . wasn't me'. Geoff told me again and again to hold my tongue. Norman Hunter's mum used to lash out with her handbag when people booed her Norman.

JUDITH HURST, wife of Geoff, in Brian James, *Journey to Wembley*, **1977**.

HE's not going to join Pisa for the simple and most important reason that his mother decided that days ago.

BRIAN CLOUGH on son Nigel, **1988**.

To suggest a player shouldn't have sex the night before a match is the height of silliness. I've had enjoyable nights and mornings before a game and it never affected me. But before a match I won't put a lot of energy into it.

GRAEME SOUNESS, Rangers player-manager, **1985**.

A lot of beautiful girls may be made available to you before the game. Such traps are aimed at destabilizing you. You are going to war and must be on the lookout for all kinds of weapons.

KING MTETWA, Swaziland Home Affairs minister, to Highlanders FC before game in Lesotho, **1985**.

MIND you, if Rod Stewart can't pull the best-looking girls in the world, what chance do the rest of us have?

MAURICE JOHNSTON, Nantes and Scotland striker, in *Mo – The Autobiography*, **1988**.

I hope they will be waiting for me at the airport where I will attempt to satisfy them.

SERGINHO of Brazil on being voted, by Brazilian women, 'Most attractive player' in **1982** World Cup.

HE leaves pregnant women on every street corner.

JOSEPH-LUIS NUNEZ, Barcelona president, on the Real Madrid player Juanito, **1982**. The remark caused a defamation suit.

THE Italians are a gayer set of lads who love life, and their girlfriends. Especially their girlfriends – if one is to judge from the many conversations I've overheard on football grounds all over the country. They think the English boys are slightly mad putting sport before the ladies.

EDDIE FIRMANI, on his transfer from Charlton to Sampdoria, in *Football with the Millionaires*, **1960**.

HE [the Italian footballer] gets mobbed by the girls with all the zest which seems to follow Johnny Ray around the world, and there are times when these young ladies become a nuisance and ought to be spanked and sent home to bed.

EDDIE FIRMANI, as above.

NEARLY 800 girl readers wrote in during the close season to say that Gerry Bridgwood of Stoke City was the most attractive man in League football.

FOOTBALL LEAGUE REVIEW, **1967**.

WHEN women will stand (as they do) for unlimited time with the rain pelting down upon her clothes, ruining her hat and her comfort, it shows an interest amounting almost to heroism.

MONICA'S MIRROR column, *Leicester Mercury*, in an article headed 'Women Thrilled by Football – Quite Under its Sway', **1923**.

I recently met Jimmy Hill who argues for football as a family game. When I actually spoke to him, his reaction was polite but uninterested.

JILL TOWNSEND, girlfriend of musician Alan Price (then a Fulham director), **1981**.

Do you know that the thing managers dread is a player's wife becoming pregnant? It affects their game . . . a player gets worried and he loses form. A woman manager might be in a position to set his mind at rest about things and a whole host of other domestic difficulties like bust-ups with girlfriends.

JILL TOWNSEND, **1981**.

To score in front of 70,000 fans at San Siro is like finding a place in a woman's heart. No, it's better.

NICOLA BERTI, Inter Milan scorer, **1988**.

BLIMEY, you're the first bird I've met with an FA coaching badge.

RON ATKINSON to woman journalist who asked about Sheffield Wednesday's long-ball game under his predecessors, **1989**.

IT is as plain as can be that football does not come within the Equal Opportunities Act.

LORD DENNING, Master of the Rolls, on the Appeal Court's refusal to overturn decision to stop twelve-year-old Theresa Bennett from playing for a boys' club in the **1970s**.

WOMEN should be in the kitchen, the discotheque and the boutique but not in football.

RON ATKINSON, Sheffield Wednesday manager, **1989**.

8

We Are The People

To go to the match was to escape from the dark of despondency into the light of combat. Here, by association with the home team, positive identity could be claimed in muscle and goals. To win was a personal success, to lose another clout from life. Football was not so much an opiate of the masses as a flag run up against the gaffer bolting his gates and the landlord armed with his bailiffs.

ARTHUR HOPCRAFT in *The Football Man*, **1968**.

MOST people are in a factory from nine till five. Their job may be to turn out 263 little circles. At the end of the week they're three short and somebody has a go at them. On Saturday afternoons they deserve something to go and shout at.

RODNEY MARSH, **1967**.

FANS see clubs spending millions on players while they're expected to pay £1 for a programme. They see executive boxes being installed while they're peeing down each other's legs in scruffy, inadequate toilets. They read about huge sponsorship deals while they are drinking stewed tea and paying more for a stale piece of cake than they paid last year.

GRAHAM TAYLOR, Aston Villa manager, **1988**.

I venture to suggest the turn has come of the public who bring the grist to the mill. Why not covered accommodation for spectators, dry ground to stand on, and a reduced admission if possible. The profits will stand it. Many a wreath has been purchased by standing on wet ground on Saturday afternoons.

LETTER signed A.M.H., *Birmingham Mail*, March **1905**.

A northern horde of uncouth garb and strange oaths.

PALL MALL GAZETTE on Blackburn Rovers fans in London for the **1884** Cup final.

THERE is no real local interest to excuse the frenzy of the mob, since the players come from all over the kingdom, and may change their clubs each season.

C. B. FRY'S MAGAZINE on crowd trouble, **1906**.

THAT Association Football is becoming notorious for scenes and disgraceful exhibitions of ruffianism. That the rabble will soon make it impossible for law-abiding citizens to attend matches.

SCOTTISH ATHLETIC JOURNAL article headed 'Things Worth Knowing', **1887**.

A very large proportion of the Crystal Palace crowd [for the FA Cup final] is composed of provincials who travel, many of them, by night excursions from various grimy manufacturing centres in the North and Midlands, being dumped down in the heart of London when the streets are almost deserted.

PICKFORD AND GIBSON, **1906**.

THOUGH they were all very excited they conducted themselves with as much decorum as if they had been millionaires, except that they showed more impatience over the slowness of the train.

PASTIME magazine's description of 1000 Luton supporters arriving at King's Cross en route for Millwall, **1905**.

I got the ball in the middle of the field and a voice out of the centre stand shouted out, 'Give it to Taylor.' So I gave it to Taylor. Five minutes afterwards, I got the ball again in the middle of the field and the same voice shouted, 'Give it to Matthews.' So I gave it to Matthews. A couple of minutes later, I got the ball again, but this time there were three Arsenal players around me so I looked up at the stand and the voice came back, 'Use your own discretion.'

STAN MORTENSEN, Blackpool and England player, in Robin Daniels, *Blackpool Football*, **1972**.

ON Saturday evenings the Barnsley streets became a sea of 'Green 'Uns' as the fanatics read the *Sheffield Star* reports. They met their wives and, depending on their mood after the match, took a night on the town, perhaps a meal at the bus-station cafe, or a visit to one of the eight cinemas or a dance-hall. Occasionally a man could be seen reading the 'Green 'Un' behind his partner's back as they waltzed.

ALISTER & WARD in *Barnsley – A Study in Football, 1953–59.*

To me, the youngsters who wait patiently – often for hours in the rain – with a well-kept autograph book are to be commended. Firstly they have adopted a hobby which does nobody any harm. Secondly they are taking an interest in football – how much better than those who a short time ago were concerned in the 'Rock 'n' Roll Riots'.

BILLY WRIGHT, Wolves and England captain, in *Football is my Passport*, **1959**.

CHANTS rather than just plain cheering are much more popular on the Continent. If the fans in Britain kept to their 'Two, four, six, eight. Who do we appreciate?' or their 'One, two, three, four. Who is it that we are for?' they would come into line with the Continental fan, who likes chanting and applauding rather than what he might call the 'undisciplined' cheering of the British.

JOHN CHARLES, Juventus and Wales, in *The Gentle Giant*, **1962**.

THE real trouble with our national team is that in Italy we have fifty million advisers.

GIANNI RIVERA, Milan and Italy, **1969**.

As a boy I genuinely believed in the man who never ate bacon because its red and white stripes reminded him of Sheffield United – indeed in my blue and white Wednesday heart I applauded and supported his loyalty.

ROY HATTERSLEY MP in *Goodbye to Yorkshire*, **1976**.

THERE are times when, as a guest in the boardroom of some mighty
First League club, I find that the Third Division results are not read
out – they stop at the Second Division. Then it is that I face superior
smiles or the loud laughs and ask, with my heart in my mouth,
anxious as ever, 'How did Reading get on?'

JOHN ARLOTT from *Concerning Soccer*, **1950**, Arlott cycled sixteen miles each way
from his Hampshire home to support Reading as a boy.

ANY man who is paid to serve his country . . . should never try and
gain financially. That may be to you a very old-fashioned idea. But
I'm very patriotic at every level. I adore my county cricket team
(Somerset) and my football team, because I support the greatest
football team in England, Bristol Rovers.

JEFFREY ARCHER, author-politician, during *Spycatcher* case, **1987**.

MY great heroes are Sir Stanley Matthews and Dave Beasant.

JUNE WHITFIELD, comedy actress and Wimbledon fan, **1988**.

I'D like to have been born Bob Latchford and then become Nye
Bevan when I was too old to play football.

DEREK HATTON, Everton fan and former Liverpool councillor, **1988**.

I collected Chelsea programmes for years, took them to New York
with me when I moved there. But when I arrived and opened the
trunk I'd packed them in I discovered they'd all been stolen. It was
very sad.

VIDAL SASSOON, hairdresser millionaire, **1988**.

I can remember taking my seat at Hampden before a Scotland
match and being picked out by a spectator who was obviously not a
Celtic supporter. 'McGrain, ya Fenian b——!' he shouted up at me
before he realized the description was inaccurate and changed his
insult to 'McGrain, ya diabetic b——!'

DANNY MCGRAIN, non-Catholic, diabetic ex-Celtic defender, in Hugh Keevins,
Celtic Greats, **1988**.

WHO are the people?
We arra people!

RANGERS fans' call-response chant.

I just wish there were 10,000 more in the ground chanting for my
blood.

LEN WALKER, Aldershot manager, on demonstration by fifty fans after home defeat
by Hartlepool, **1983**.

WITH a small crowd like we had today, you can hear them all
shouting. It's not very pleasant but I can understand them. It's their
club, after all.

BOBBY CAMPBELL, Fulham manager, after home defeat by Oxford, **1980**.

WE were disappointed we couldn't play on Saturday because we had
supporters travelling from all over the country. There was one
coming from London, one from Newcastle, one from
Brighton. . . .

DAVID KILPATRICK, Rochdale chairman, on the postponement of FA Cup tie at
Manchester United, **1986**.

IT's gone now, mainly because of hooliganism. I wouldn't dare walk
about now, in my old outfit, in another town. They'd be after me,
wouldn't they? Around 1963, I could feel that some spectators were
getting out of hand.

SYD BEVERS, leader of the 'Atomic Boys', a group of Blackpool fans who went to
matches in fancy-dress in the **1950s**.

THE club call us hooligans, but who'd cheer them if we didn't come?
You have to stand there and take it when Spurs are losing and the
others are jeering at you. It's not easy. We support them everywhere and we get no thanks.

SPURS FAN quoted in Hunter Davies, *The Glory Game*, **1972**.

THE Spurs fans, marching and shouting their way back to the station, banged on the windows of the coach as it threaded its way back through the crowds. 'Go on, smash the town up,' said Cyril [Knowles], encouraging them.

HUNTER DAVIES, *The Glory Game*, **1972**.

I'D like to kill all the Arsenal players and then burn the stand down.

SPURS FAN in Hunter Davies, *The Glory Game*, **1972**.

I'VE spent six years watching that b——— Walker and then he goes and scores two goals against us.

JOHN LEFTLEY, Chelsea fan arrested for trying to punch club's former winger Clive Walker of Sunderland, **1985**.

THEIR support can be an embarrassment sometimes, but I'd rather have them as an embarrassment than not at all.

TOMMY DOCHERTY on Manchester United fans, **1974**.

WHILE the name Manchester United has its advantages, the association with football connects basketball with violence and thuggery.

DICK KAY, one of consortium taking over the Manchester basketball club when United pulled out, **1988**.

THE image of the British gentleman along the Belgian coast has given way to one of truculent youths, throwing cobblestones and wielding sticks.

JEAN-MARIE BERKVENS, Belgian attorney, on rioting Manchester United fans at Ostend, **1974**.

THE Belgians have got the answer – jail them without trial, put them in a dungeon and half-starve them. That would cure Britain's soccer hooligans.

JOHN MORAN, Manchester United fan jailed in Ostend, **1974**.

THE violence was sickening. The only answer is for decent supporters – and they are in the majority – to become vigilantes on the terraces. A few thumps on the nose would soon stop these silly youngsters.

ALEC STOCK, Fulham manager, 1975.

YOU must have some sort of deterrent and the first thing I would advocate for these people is the birch. You don't stroke a wild dog, you blow his brains out.

RON SAUNDERS, Birmingham manager, after crowd violence had disrupted an FA Cup tie against West Ham, 1984.

THE most violent offenders should be flogged in front of the main stand before the start of a home game. I feel so strongly on this matter, I'd volunteer to do the whipping myself.

ALLAN CLARKE, Leeds manager, 1980.

WE can no longer call these people hooligans. It is terrorism.

JOOP VAN DER REIJDEN, Dutch Minister of Culture, after Spurs' visit to Feyenoord, 1983.

TOTTENHAM'S supporters were exemplary, the sort of guests we always like to have here.

BAYERN MUNICH official, 1983.

THERE is no doubt that Britain is a country rich in culture and tradition but its soccer envoys abroad are worse than the barbarous hordes headed by Attila.

SPANISH NEWSPAPER editorial after fights at Castilla-West Ham game, 1980.

I wish they would all be put on a boat and dropped in the ocean. We are ashamed of people like this. The Italians must think we are idiots.

RON GREENWOOD, England manager, after riots in Turin, 1980.

THE offenders should be apprehended and shipped back to England in chains.

AUSTRALIAN NEWSPAPER editorial after trouble involving English expatriates at World Youth Cup game in Sydney, **1982**.

THEY came for warfare, to cause trouble and fight. It's been said that they're a small minority. They are not. There were nearly 1700 of them and nearly all of them were at it.

BERT MILLICHIP, FA chairman, on England fans in Luxembourg, **1983**.

IT's a pity your hooligans aren't coming. We like your hooligans. We think you have the best hooligans in Europe.

GREEK TAXI DRIVER on being informed that not many England fans were visiting Salonika, **1982**.

THE ANIMALS ARE COMING

EL SOL (Monterrey) headline on the prospect of England fans' visit, **1986**.

WE do not believe there will be trouble. Because of the cost of getting here, we expect an upper middle-class sort of person, the type who represents the British tradition of education. . . . Like gentlemen, like an officer trained at Sandhurst. Someone like David Niven.

GUILLERMO URQUIGO, Monterrey Police spokesman, on the kind of English visitor he hoped for, **1986**.

THE hooligans do feel themselves to be representatives of England. They abuse foreigners and feel superior to them.

PATRICK MURPHY, Leicester University sociologist, **1988**.

YOU gotta stand by England.

ENGLAND FAN explaining why he was fighting in West Germany, **1988**.

WE'VE won two world wars, one World Cup.

ENGLAND FANS' chant in Stuttgart, **1988**.

THEY are doing what we were doing one thousand years ago.

STUTTGART POLICE spokesman on England fans' Nazi salutes, **1988**.

IT'S no worse than the English on holiday in Spain. They're better than some rugby teams I've driven, and you should see what they get up to at beer festivals. Football has got a bad name.

COACH DRIVER of England fans in Switzerland before the European Championships, **1988**.

SIR, Following the remarks made by the Minister for Sport after the arrest of the drunken brawling supporters at the England v Scotland match last Saturday, I take it he will not blame the Spanish Tourist Authority when they undoubtedly turn up on the Costa Brava and repeat it this summer.

JOE ASHTON MP in letter to *The Times*, **1988**.

A steward got stabbed outside our door. I think a lot of their problem over there is that the police don't carry guns. The fans beat up on them all the time.

BRENT GOULET, USA international striker, on his season with Bournemouth and Crewe, in *St Louis Post Dispatch*, **1988**.

YOU don't have to be an unemployed teenager to be a soccer yob. Lots of men who go to work in grey suits and earn good money also terrorize the terraces. They have fantasies about being Superman or Conan the Barbarian. Their ordinary lives make them feel stifled.

JANE FIRBANK, psychologist, **1988**.

THERE are two league tables these days, one for the club matches and the other for the supporters – who ran, when and from whom. And this second league is rooted in lower working-class standards of masculine aggression.

JOHN WILLIAMS, Leicester University sociologist, **1983**.

SOME of us live in Leeds and go around there and while it may not be the defendants, it is all those people in the public gallery staring at us and clocking us.

> JUROR at Leeds Crown Court, explaining why jury felt threatened during trial of Leeds fans in 'Operation Wild Boar', **1988**.

YOU see kids of seven or eight walking round in Everton tracksuits making V signs, swearing at you because you play for Liverpool. I feel sorry for them, who knows what they're going to become? It's sad.

> JOHN BARNES, Liverpool's black winger, **1988**.

SOME fruit and vegetable dealers did very well.

> BARNES, after being pelted with bananas during Merseyside derby, **1987**.

APPARENTLY they couldn't find one decent Millwall supporter.

> DENIS HOWELL MP, Minister for Sport, complaining about an 'irresponsible' and 'unbalanced' edition of BBC1's 'Panorama' on football hooliganism, **1977**.

REALLY good Millwall supporters, right, they can't stand their club being slagged down you know, and it all wells up, you know, and you just feel like hitting someone.

> MILLWALL FAN in Roger Ingham et al., *Football Hooliganism: The Wider Context*, **1978**.

THE Den's the friendliest place I've ever known. I'm not saying that we don't have crowd trouble, but the truth is nothing like the image the club has. The crowd is very partisan – but that is one of the things that attracted me to it.

> JOHN DOCHERTY, Millwall manager, **1988**.

OUR supporters were absolutely fantastic. If you could bottle their enthusiasm you'd make a fortune.

> DOCHERTY, defending Millwall fans after crowd trouble at Arsenal, **1988**.

THERE are dirty-mouthed and violent elements who have attached themselves to Millwall. . . . But they do not exist in a vacuum. They do not change their shape on a Saturday afternoon. A cruel and violent football hooligan is a cruel and violent hooligan full stop.

JOHN STALKER, former assistant chief constable of Manchester and crowd consultant to Millwall, **1988**.

No one likes us, we don't care.

MILLWALL fans' song, to tune of 'Sailing', **1980s**.

YOU folks may be rightly proud of your title 'Football's Fairest Crowd', but for my part I would like to see not a little but a lot more partisanship in favour of Chelsea. All too many people come to Stamford Bridge to see a football match – instead of to cheer Chelsea.

TED DRAKE, Chelsea manager, in club programme, August **1952**.

CHELSEA supporters tried to throw my 10-year-old son over a wall with a 70 foot drop. I asked someone the time and they said, 'You're Middlesbrough fans'. The next thing we knew they were coming towards us saying, 'Get those Northern bastards. Let's get the kid and throw him over the wall.' The police dived in and saved us.

DAVID BRAITHWAITE, Middlesbrough fan, after play-off match at Chelsea, **1988**.

THERE was a lot of spitting from the crowd, which is what you would expect in British football.

STEVE PERRYMAN, Brentford manager, after incident at Port Vale, **1989**.

I didn't mind the Mars bars, but I didn't fancy a big clemmy [Geordie slang for brick] bouncing off me.

CHRIS WADDLE, Tottenham midfielder, on chocolate-bar barrage against himself and Paul Gascoigne on their return to Newcastle, **1988**.

I met these football fans smoking in a non-smoker on the railway, so I said: 'Put it out . . . put it out . . . put it out.' And they did. I think they're far less dangerous than dogs.

BARBARA WOODHOUSE, TV personality and dog trainer, **1980**.

THERE are more hooligans in the House of Commons than at a football match.

BRIAN CLOUGH, **1980**.

WHAT comes next – water cannon, guards, tanks, and consultant undertakers to ferry away the dead?

SIMON TURNEY, Greater London Council, on Chelsea's proposed electric fence, **1985**.

IF this is what soccer is to become, let it die.

L'EQUIPE editorial after European Cup final disaster had claimed 39 lives, **1985**.

IF somebody is celebrating it means we still have much to learn.

GIORGIO CARDETTI, Mayor of Turin, after Juventus's win following Heysel deaths, **1985**.

I'M sure the crowd will give us all a great big hand. They are known for being such great sportsmen.

DIEGO MARADONA before playing for the World XI *v* the Football League at Wembley, where his every touch was booed, **1987**.

IN January, my wife Thelma accompanied me to the match between Dagenham and Grays Athletic. This meant she had completed visits to every ground in the Vauxhall-Opel League and we, as a married couple, have completed a set of V-OL venues. Has any other married couple achieved anything similar in the V-OL, or indeed, any other league?

LETTER to *Pyramid* non-League magazine, **1989**.

MY favourite [letter received] is one which said, 'You . . . Smith
. . . Jones and Heighway had better keep looking over your
shoulder. You are going to get your dews.'

EMLYN HUGHES in Brian James, *Journey to Wembley*, **1977**.

THEY tend to start off with things like 'Dear Stupid' or 'Dear Big
Head'. One man wrote to me, beginning 'Dear Alfie Boy'.

SIR ALF RAMSEY on letters he received after internationals, in Arthur Hopcraft, *The
Football Man*, **1968**.

AFTER three games this season, I know my club Birmingham City
are going to be relegated. Is this a record?

LETTER to *Sunday People*, **1977**.

JUST about the only point worth remembering about Port Vale's
match with Hereford on Monday evening was the fact that the
attendance figure, 2744, is a perfect cube, 14 × 14 × 14.

LETTER to Stoke *Evening Sentinel*, **1979**.

SUNDERLAND'S Barry Venison once autographed my head.
My mother once bumped into Oxford's Garry Briggs in Tescos.
The best man at my grandfather's wedding was the father-in-law of
Middlesbrough manager Willie Maddren.

LETTERS from readers to 'Claim To Fame' in *Match* magazine, **1985**.

THE Spion Kop at Liverpool is famous, as certain football reporters
have discovered when an ill-chosen word in their writings has
brought upon their heads a storm of abuse from 'behind the goal'.
That Anfield Spion Kop is one of Liverpool Football Club's prized
possessions, and in all seriousness, I am certain matches have been
won through the vocal efforts of its regular patrons.

MATT BUSBY, ex-Liverpool player, in *My Story*, **1957**.

THE Giro Cup final.

MERSEYSIDE fan on Liverpool *v* Everton Milk Cup final, **1984**.

I'VE seen a Goal Scored Against Liverpool.
I've Seen Liverpool Beaten.

> LIVERPOOL supporters' badges during the record-equalling 29-game unbeaten start, **1987–88**.

MAGGIE isn't the only one with Crooks at No. 11.

> SPURS banner at civic reception after FA Cup victory, **1981**.

DEVONSHIRE'S the cream, Rice is the pudding.

> WEST HAM banner at FA Cup final v Arsenal, **1980**.

COMMUNISM v Alcoholism.

> SCOTTISH banner at Soviet Union v Scotland World Cup match, **1982**.

DON'T worry lads. Ally MacLeod's in Blackpool.

> SCOTTISH banner in Seville, **1982**.

THE Boys from the Blue Stuff.

> EVERTON banner, Milk Cup final v Liverpool, **1984**.

MANCHESTER – A Trophy-Free Zone.

> BANNER at Liverpool v Everton, FA Cup final, **1986**.

No Valley, No Validity.

> CHARLTON banner at last match before move to Crystal Palace, **1985**.

QUEREMOS Frijoles No Goles (We want beans not goals).

> MEXICAN STEELWORKERS' banner at the opening ceremony, World Cup, **1986**.

GARY Wager is safer than a condom.

> MERTHYR TYDFIL banner in Bergamo, Italy in praise of their goalkeeper, **1987**.

PETER Shilton, Peter Shilton, does your missus know you're here?

ARSENAL NORTH BANK to Nottingham Forest goalkeeper after revelation that he had been caught in a compromising position late at night, **1980**.

STEVE Foster, Steve Foster, what a difference you have made.

MANCHESTER UNITED fans' song at Wembley Cup final replay, **1984**. Brighton captain Foster didn't play in the first match which ended 2–2. United won the replay 4–0.

Two Gary Stevens, there's only two Gary Stevens . . .

ENGLAND FANS' song in Mexico City, **1986**.

YOU'RE so bad you're worse than Aldershot.

READING fans taunting Luton during 4–1 Simod Cup win at Wembley, **1988**.

ARE you watching, Liverpool?

TRANMERE fans revelling in their team's success in the League centenary tournament at Wembley, **1988**.

BRIAN Moore's Head Looks Uncannily Like London Planetarium

GILLINGHAM fanzine title, **1988**. Moore is a former Gills director.

AND Smith Must Score!

BRIGHTON fanzine title, named after Gordon Smith's last-minute miss in 1983 FA Cup final, **1988**.

SING When We're Fishing

GRIMSBY fanzine title, **1988**.

ELM Park Disease

READING fanzine title, **1988**.

A kick up the Rs

QUEEN'S PARK RANGERS fanzine title, **1988**.

MOST players hate the fanzines. They tend to be critical of footballers and the way the game is run. Professional players are very wary of anything that makes fun of them. They can be absurdly loyal to the good image of the game.

PAT NEVIN, Chelsea and Scotland winger, **1988**.

THE next goal wins it!

LEEDS FANS' chant when their team trailed 7–1 at Stoke, **1986**.

TODAY's attendance 22,451. And 7,000 bananas!

ELECTRONIC scoreboard at Manchester City at height of craze for fans to carry 'inflatables', **1989**.

BORN St Luke's Hospital, 24 Jan, within sight of the hallowed turf. Legs like Jimmy Scoular.

BIRTH announcement in *Telegraph & Argus* by Bradford Park Avenue diehard – 14 years after club folded, **1988**.

YOU lose some, you draw some.

JASPER CARROT, comedian, on supporting Birmingham City, **1978**.

SUPPORTER: A fiver on Celtic tae beat Arsenal.
WORKER: Sorry sir, we don't take bets on friendlies.
SUPPORTER: Celtic dinnae play friendlies. . . .

EXCHANGE in Islington bookmaker's before Arsenal *v* Celtic testimonial, **1980**.

THEIR ability to smuggle drink into matches makes Papillon look like a learner.

SCOTTISH POLICE FEDERATION spokesman, **1981**.

IT may have been an awful night, but the meat and potato pies were brill.

'AWAY TRAVELLER' in the Crewe Alexandra Supporters Association newsletter, on a visit to Halifax, **1983**.

IT's bad enough to have to go and watch Bristol City without having things stolen.

JUDGE DESMOND VOWDEN QC, sentencing man who stole from a City fan's car, **1984**.

To go on and on the way they did . . . amazing. They deserved a result.

LENNIE LAWRENCE, Charlton manager, on fans' Back-to-the-Valley campaign, **1989**.

THERE's a new breed of flash young executives who think they've got the right to call to account anybody in the world.

RON GREENWOOD after the Wembley crowd had booed his side against Spain, **1981**.

AT least Joe Public has been very good to me. You know, he's a damned nice fella.

BOBBY ROBSON, replying to media criticism, **1988**.

IT is the culmination of all my dreams to see the Qemal Stadium in Tirana.

ATTILA THE STOCKBROKER, poet-ranter, before leaving for Albania v England, **1989**.

Tifozë futbolli Britanikë dergojmë paqesore u dergojme shokëve tamë shqiptarë vëllazërore me rastine takimit të parë midis dy kombeve tona.
(Friendly British football fans salute their Albanian comrades on the occasion of the first football match between our two countries.)

T-SHIRT slogan on England supporters' trip to Tirana, **1989**.

9

The Fourth Estate

Press

IT is high time our newspapers (or at any rate those from the *Daily Mail* up) stopped filling their back pages with pictures of repulsively ugly football players and gave news from the stately homes, decorated by photographs of them in the changing seasons explained by Mr Glyn Boyd-Hart, preferably with a gardenia in his button-hole.

AUBERON WAUGH, the *Independent*, **1989**.

IT'LL be tits, bums, QPR and roll your own fags.

DEREK JAMESON's editorial vision for his new *Daily Star*, **1979**.

HE is to the point with the pen as with the tongue, and calls a football 'the ball'. Such things as 'inflated spheres', 'tegumentary cylinders', and the 'leather globe' he leaves to others. . . . He does not deal in superlatives nor is he led to place the football player of momentary eminence on a pedestal.

PICKFORD AND GIBSON, **1906**, on J. J. Bentley, 'Doyen of Journalists', ex-Bolton secretary, FA vice-president and League president.

ONE or two Glasgow papers used to employ pigeons, and a few country papers still do; but the pigeon is a slow, clumsy and uncertain messenger. Practically all the up-to-date papers now use a telephone for local reports.

PICKFORD AND GIBSON, **1906**.

No club official likes the type of correspondent who constantly seeks information from players by visiting their homes or ringing them up on the telephone at all hours. These are the hole-and-corner methods of the few to which we take exception.

BOB LORD, Burnley chairman, on why he had barred journalists from the press-box, in *My Fight for Football*, **1963**.

ALTHOUGH I'm only human and do not always agree with sentiments expressed by writers, I'm wise enough, I hope, to appreciate that the spectator sees more of a match than a player, and I can often learn a good deal by studying some of the reporters' comments.

ALF RAMSEY, the player, **1950s**.

I have to make a living just like you. I happen to make mine in a nice way – you happen to make yours in a nasty way.

SIR ALF RAMSEY to journalists in **1973**.

REPORTERS want a quick answer to something I might need all Saturday night and all Sunday to get somewhere near.

HOWARD WILKINSON, Sheffield Wednesday manager, **1983**.

STRICTLY off the record, no comment.

COLIN MURPHY, Lincoln manager, **1983**.

ALF Ramsey was being crucified by the Press when I started and now I am about to leave it is Bobby Robson's turn.

TED CROKER on retirement as FA secretary, **1989**.

PRESSURE? You people [the media] supply the pressure. If you didn't exist my job would be twice as easy and twice as pleasurable.

BOBBY ROBSON in Mexico City, **1985**.

I have been let down so often, read so much that wasn't remotely true, that I now find it difficult to trust anyone who shows up with notebook and pen.

JOHN HOLLINS, Chelsea manager, **1988**.

HE could be better employed writing the Noddy books for Enid Blyton.

KEN BATES, Chelsea chairman, on reporter, **1989**.

NOT only do they know nothing about football, but if you were to shut them up in a room by themselves they couldn't even write a letter to mother.

CESAR MENOTTI, Argentina's manager, on his country's soccer journalists, **1982**.

THEATRE critics and film critics do know what the mechanics of a production are. Most football writers don't. So players tend to despise journalists. On the other hand players are flattered by their attention. Flattered by the idea that this guy has come along especially to write about them. So you have contempt and at the same time a slight awe at seeing your name in print.

EAMON DUNPHY in *Only a Game?*, **1976**.

A lot of people in football don't have much time for the press: they say they're amateurs. But I say to those people, 'Noah built the ark, but the Titanic was built by professionals.'

MALCOLM ALLISON, **1980**.

NICE to see all you Press lads here. It's Hartlepool next week, so I suppose it will be back to badgering the *Ilford Recorder* for a bit of space.

FRANK CLARK, Leyton Orient manager, after FA Cup defeat by Nottingham Forest, **1988**.

THEY were Rotherham fellers, writing in a Rotherham paper, for other Rotherham fellers, so bugger impartiality.

BILL GRUNDY, journalist, in *Foul!*, **1975**.

HALF an hour? You could shoot Ben Hur in half an hour. You've got 15 seconds.

RON ATKINSON, Manchester United manager, to photographer who asked for 30 minutes with him, **1984**.

MR Stanley Heathman, married with five children, said that they had never been in doubt they would be liberated. It was just a matter of how and when. He astonished one soldier by asking: 'Can you tell me – have Leeds been relegated?'

POOLED DISPATCH by journalists during Falklands War, **1982**.

THE accused claimed he was the reincarnated brother of Conan the Barbarian, that he was turning into an elk and had played for Leeds United. A defence psychiatrist said he was mad.

DAILY TELEGRAPH court report, **1988**.

JUST before the end O'Donnell banged a fierce shot against the underside of the crossbar and an eagle-eyed linesman announced that a goal had been scored. Arsenal could hardly have been more indignant had they been told the goal counted four, that Preston had won the match, the championship, the FA Cup, Doggetts Coat and Badge, and the Open Golf championship, and that the Arsenal team would have to carry their bags to the station.

N. J. N. DIXON, *Manchester Guardian*, **1930s**.

BY and by the scoreboard was a lying jade on Saturday. It told us that City were losing 0–2 at half-time. Homes have been broken up by lesser rumours.

N. J. N. DIXON, *Manchester Guardian*, **1939**.

SEE Naples and Dai.

DESMOND HACKETT in *Daily Express* with Bangor City in Italy, **1962**.

Mr Martinez [referee] was slow to realize that the Dutch invented the clog.

DAVID LACEY in the *Guardian* on the World Cup match between Holland and Italy, **1978**.

Queen in brawl at Palace

GUARDIAN headline, **1970**. Crystal Palace had a forward called Gerry Queen.

The end of the world!

SUN headline after England failed to qualify for World Cup finals, **1973**.

Savages! Animals!

DAILY MIRROR headline after weekend of terrace violence, **1975**.

Arsenal: A Nation Mourns

GUARDIAN headline after Arsenal's FA Cup defeat at Everton ensured they would not make a fourth successive final appearance, **1981**.

O Nosse Futebol E Como A Nossa Inflacco . . . 100% (Our Football is Like Our Inflation . . . 100%)

JORNAL DA TARDE (Sao Paolo) headline after Brazil's win over England, **1981**.

Argies Smashed!

SUN headline after Argentina's defeat by Belgium, World Cup **1982**.

Irish frivolity masks both fitness and resolve

TIMES headline, World Cup **1982**.

Orrible little Basten

SUN headline after Van Basten's hat-trick for Holland *v* England, **1988**.

In the name of God, go!

DAILY MIRROR headline directive to Bobby Robson, **1988**.

Plonker

SUN headline after England's 0-0 draw with Sweden, **1988**. In his press conference
Robson had called Sweden Denmark

For the love of Allah, go!

DAILY MIRROR headline after England's 1-1 draw *v* Saudi Arabia, **1988**.

Saxton signing is first of few

NORTHERN ECHO headline, **1988**.

Little to report as Dale crash

ROCHDALE OBSERVER headline, **1989**. The report, on 4-0 defeat by Scunthorpe,
ran to 28 paragraphs.

I'll expect nine out of ten in the *People*.

KENNY DALGLISH, after coming on as 87th-minute substitute for Liverpool *v*
Wimbledon, **1988**.

Given supreme power I'd clip the wings of the Press barons. I'd get rid of the Fleet Street bosses and form workers' co-operatives. How this could be achieved I'm not so sure . . .

PAT NEVIN, Chelsea winger, in *Media Week*, **1986**.

Television

There are people on the pitch . . . they think it's all over (*Hurst completes hat-trick*) . . . It is now!

KENNETH WOLSTENHOLME, BBC commentator, at the end of World Cup final, **1966**.

IT's only ten inches tall, it's solid gold – and it means England have won the World Cup.

WOLSTENHOLME, **1966**.

PRODUCERS started putting pressure on commentators to generate more excitement. And the trend began of over-intellectualizing the game. Football can't be dissected like a symphony. It's the game of the masses, and arguing about it is one of its attractions.

WOLSTENHOLME on the change in commentating styles which left him behind, **1988**.

IT was when old ladies who had been coming into my shop for years started talking about sweepers and creating space that I really understood the influence of television.

JACK TAYLOR, referee, **1974**.

FOOTBALL on TV on a Sunday afternoon is an entertainment. I have a duty to my employers to present as entertaining a programme as possible – not just for committed football fans, but for the guy in the street and for Mum.

BRIAN MOORE, 'The Big Match' presenter, **1975**.

THE liberties you people take are unbelievable. You TV people seem to think you are entitled to intrude wherever and whenever you want.

RON GREENWOOD, England manager, ordering cameras out of team's HQ before match, **1981**.

WELL that's the magic of television, isn't it? You hype up the sound a bit, point the camera where the crowd is thickest, cut out all the boring rubbish, and you've got The Big Match.

TED AYLING, 'The Big Match' director, **1982**.

IT's our policy to show the better side of the game. It's not censorship, it's selectivity.

BOB ABRAHAMS, 'Match of the Day' editor, explaining why the violence in a Birmingham *v* Watford FA Cup match had been cut, **1984**.

WE want football to tell us exactly what they would like in the ideal world and then, I'd assume, we will tell them what they can have.

JOHN BROMLEY, Head of ITV Sport, **1982**.

WHEN the League offered us thirty-one matches 'live', we said: 'Can you deliver?' The answer was: 'Anything can be delivered, so long as the money's right.' I was shattered that they could believe that money is more important than the welfare of the game.

CLIFF MORGAN, BBC Head of Outside Broadcasts, **1983**.

I'M sure the top clubs would be magnanimous and give some of the money to the small clubs, but it's essential that we keep the lion's share.

DOUGLAS ALEXIOU, Spurs chairman, on the threat of breakaway negotiations with television by the big clubs, **1983**.

I don't watch television myself. But my family do and they tell me the most popular programmes are the ones which are full of violence. On that basis football ought to do rather well.

JACK DUNNETT, Football League president, **1985**.

IN one sense soccer is like religion. It must be witnessed in the place of worship.

BOB WALL, Arsenal secretary, after 7,483 had watched Scotland *v* Northern Ireland at Hampden – and 13 million on TV, **1969**.

I should rather like the Match of the Day theme tune played at my funeral.

CARDINAL BASIL HUME, Newcastle United fan, **1986**.

10

He Who Must Be Obeyed

THEN my eyesight started to go, and I took up refereeing.

NEIL MIDGLEY, FA Cup final referee, **1987**.

THE trouble with referees is that they know the rules but they don't know the game.

BILL SHANKLY during referees' clampdown on dirty play, **1971**.

PEOPLE say we've got the best referees in the world – I shudder to think what the rest are like.

MANCHESTER UNITED DEFENDER, **1973**.

WE had a Mauritian referee against Paraguay. Mauritius is a lovely island, but they don't play football.

EVARISTO MACEDA, Iraqi coach, World Cup, **1986**.

THERE was a murderer on the pitch – the referee.

OMAR BORRAS, Uruguay manager, on the Italian official who sent off one of his defenders after 40 seconds *v* Scotland, World Cup, **1986**.

BLOODY English referees.

BERT TRAUTMANN, Manchester City's German goalkeeper, after being sent off *v* West Ham, **1962**.

There was a chap who couldn't run
Whose playing days were long since done;
And consequently he was free
To rule the game as referee.
A referee can't be too old
While he has strength to take the gold;
Perhaps he cannot run or see
But all the same he'll referee.

J. H. JONES from poem, 'The Age of Referees', *c.* **1900**.

To 'referee'! To regulate the game,
To earn expenses and a guinea fee!
Yes! There is great attraction in the name
    of Referee.
Yet troublous times might be in store for me,
Did I allow the visitors a claim!
A brickbat in the eye or damaged knee,
Enough to make me permanently lame,
On second thoughts, then I decline to be –
(Although, of course, I thank you all the same)
        – A Referee.

ANONYMOUS, *c.* **1890s**.

REFEREES should arrive by the back door and leave by the back door.

ALAN HARDAKER, Football League secretary, **1960s**.

I'VE been booked now over fifty times, but never for fouling, always for dissent. I've seen players really go in to hurt people, and the referee does nothing. I haven't got a good word for any of them. I don't think they control this kind of tackling nearly enough. The newspapers say they've clamped down on it, but they haven't really.

STAN BOWLES, QPR and England midfield player, **1976**.

I'VE been one of the victims of the referee's get-tough policies. Their new approach is a joke and has affected my game.

IAN WOOD, Aldershot defender, retiring at the age of twenty-five to become . . . a butcher, **1982**.

THERE'S no rapport with referees these days. If you say anything you get booked, and if you don't they send you off for dumb insolence.

JACK CHARLTON, **1983**.

IT's getting to the stage where we hate them and they dislike us.

KENNY SANSOM, Arsenal and England left-back, on referees, **1983**.

AFTER the match an official asked for two of my players to take a dope test. I offered him the referee.

TOMMY DOCHERTY after 5–1 defeat by Brighton relegated Wolves to the Third Division, **1985**.

MOST referees see everything that goes on; a good ref is one that doesn't chicken out. A good ref is the one who'll give a penalty at Anfield against Liverpool.

DAVID CROSS, Coventry City striker, in Gordon Hill, *Give a Little Whistle*, **1975**.

HE [Charlton's John Humphrey] told me that when I saw the video I would know that the offence was committed outside the penalty area. I told him that when he watched it, he would see himself being booked.

DARRYL REEVES on awarding a penalty in his last match, at Chelsea, **1988**.

HE drives you spare sometimes . . . with Clive you are just playing to one man's rules and you don't know what's happening.

GRAHAM TAYLOR, Watford manager, on Clive 'The Book' Thomas, **1982**.

(ARTHUR) Ellis is the official who, ignoring my remarks of 'terrible decision' several times during a match, waited till I had missed an open goal, then ran past saying 'terrible shot'.

LEN SHACKLETON in *Clown Prince of Soccer*, **1955**.

SOMETIMES you have to stamp your authority on a game, but I went a bit too far.

ANDY SENNETT, Cheshire referee banned for swearing at a schoolboy player, **1988**.

THE basic training of referees is appalling. When I started as a referee, they tested my eyesight by getting me to stand at one end of a small room, facing a Bukta wall chart showing red, yellow and blue football kits. Some guy pointed to one shirt and said 'What colour's that?' I replied 'Red' and he said 'You're in.'

GORDON HILL, Football League referee, in *Give a Little Whistle*, **1975**.

I have nothing against the visually handicapped as such. Yet I am surprised they are allowed to referee at this level.

THE SOUP, Kidderminster Harriers fanzine, **1989**.

'REFEREE, what would you do if I called you a bastard?' one player inquired politely. 'I'd send you off,' I replied. 'What would you do if I thought you were a bastard?' was the next question. 'There's not a lot I could do,' I answered. 'In that case, ref, I think you're a bastard,' he said, turning smartly on his heel.

PAT PARTRIDGE, in *Oh, Ref!*, **1979**.

I got the impression that few toilets were used more than those in the referee's room.

JACK TAYLOR, World Cup referee, in *World Soccer Referee*, **1976**.

I hate Saturdays off. I'd rather take a village game than stay at home. It's that sort of gut feeling that distinguishes the referee from all the other breeds. Money doesn't come into it. If it did I would never have blown a whistle in my life.

PAT PARTRIDGE, League referee, in *Oh Ref!*, **1979**.

I tried to be professional, but the occasion got to me. I could say football is not what it was and I'm glad to be getting out, but the truth is I'm still in love with the game and will miss it dreadfully.

COLIN SEEL after his final game as League referee, **1987**.

I love football but I have my wife and family to support, and I can't do that from a hospital bed.

MALCOLM IBBOTSON, League linesman, after resigning because of 'increasing violence', **1988**.

WE may be useless, but we're not cheats.

DAVID ELLERAY, referee, to Arsenal defender Tony Adams who had called him a 'f—— cheat', **1989**.

11
Agents of Fortunes

AGENTS do nothing for the good of football. I'd like to see them lined up against a wall and machine-gunned . . . some accountants and solicitors with them.

GRAHAM TAYLOR, Watford manager, **1983**.

IT used to be the wives who affected players, now it's the agents.

BOBBY GOULD, Wimbledon manager, **1988**.

SAM Hammam [Wimbledon chairman] told me, 'You'll spread like a cancer through my club – I've got ill-educated lads at Wimbledon but they'll be educated by you.'

ERIC HALL, players' agent, **1988**.

I have no morals when it comes to dealing with my clients. I would deal with the devil to get the best deal for them.

HALL, **1989**.

BEFORE the year 2000, I'll have 50 football millionaires on my books. That's being conservative.

JOHNNY MAC, agent, **1989**.

I publicly thank God for that one.

JON SMITH, agent, on his Maradona contract, **1988**.

OUR success in the FA Cup is something to be shared by everyone in the town and not sold to the highest bidder.

PETER MORRIS, Kettering manager, following fellow giant-killers Sutton United in announcing no truck with agents, **1989**.

FOOTBALL is for everybody and not just for those newspapers who are prepared to pay money for articles.

BOBBY GOULD after intervening on journalist's behalf when an agent (Eric Hall) refused an interview, **1988**.

AFTER that we're now expecting an offer from Melchester Rovers.

BILL MCMURDO, agent to Maurice Johnston, after Scotland striker's two goals *v* France, **1989**.

MANAGERS often try to do the dirty. They make a deal with each other on the phone and tell the player to cut me out of the talks. Those who do only suffer from short-sightedness, because in a couple of months the players find out who's earning what and is back knocking on the manager's door.

JOHNNY MAC, **1989**.

So many people want an illicit slice of the action. The money has to be disguised, lost, spread around. The chairman of ICI doesn't need to talk through agents when he meets the chairman of another company to talk business. Football has them because the game's full of people on the make.

CHARLES ROBERTS, former agent to Ian Rush, **1989**.

I'M the best. I'm an egomaniac. If my phone doesn't ring for half an hour I phone the GPO and demand to know what's wrong with it.

ERIC HALL, **1989**.

They Also Serve

I never go to bed until I know where every player is when we're on tour. I'm not a spy nor a headmaster, but I do care about my players and their health.

VERNON EDWARDS, England team doctor, **1983**.

WE'VE found out from this psychiatrist that players who are friends pass to each other more.

MALCOLM ALLISON, **1973**.

ALWAYS in uniform, fraying in one or two places, and shoes in need of a quick polish. Face like a bag of chisels, moustache an essential part of the make-up in order to twitch as you approach him.

FRED EYRE, former player with twenty League and non-League teams, on club commissionaires in *Another Breath of Fred Eyre*, **1982**.

MY mind goes back to the 'glory days' at the club, when it was arranged for a certain photographer to photograph me with the players. While waiting for the training session to end he tried to persuade me to wear shorts and jersey and boots. I naturally refused and, when the players became available, he asked them to try and persuade me to get changed. Imagine my joy when one of the senior players remarked, 'Mr Jackson is our chaplain, not our mascot.'

REVEREND JOHN JACKSON, chaplain to Leeds United, in the Methodist Church Home Mission Report, **1984**.

WITH the dominance of television, the influence of sponsors, the interference of manufacturers, public-relations officers and entre-preneurs, I see no future for sport at top level. It is not too alarming a glimpse into the future to see professional football playing to empty stadia for the benefit of TV and the football pools.

SIR DENIS FOLLOWS, chairman of the British Olympic Association, **1983**.

WE are pulling out because FADS is an upright and clean company. That is something which can no longer be said about soccer. It is a sick sport. We would rather sponsor netball.

MALCOLM STANLEY, managing director of FADS, the decorating retailers, ending deal with Charlton, **1982**.

SPONSORS! They'll be wanting to pick the team next.

BOB PAISLEY, **1981**.

THE first half of this match was so bad that at half-time the sponsors asked for their ball back.

LEN SHACKLETON in press report.

SOME police officers unfortunately use Saturday as the day when they are let off the leash.

JOHN STALKER, Millwall consultant and former assistant chief constable of Manchester, **1988**.

IT was a complete balls-up all round. Half of us were drafted in at a moment's notice without being briefed. Our people were getting hurt because that lot [glancing at senior officers] got it wrong.

POLICE SERGEANT on duty at riot following Chelsea v Middlesbrough match, **1988**.

EVERYONE seems to think it must be terribly glamorous and exciting to rub down John Fashanu or Vinny Jones's legs, but I can tell you it's damned hard work.

CAROLINE BROUWER, Wimbledon physiotherapist, **1988**.

THE job has been increasingly interfered with by various authorities, whether it is police, firemen or Maggie Thatcher.

GORDON BENNETT on resigning as West Brom secretary, **1989**.

12

Political Footballs

The Super League

THE Super League idea has about as much chance of getting through as there is of Arthur Scargill admitting he needs a wig.

ERNIE CLAY, Fulham chairman, **1982**.

WHAT chance have you got when the League president is chairman of Notts County? They average 8000 a match. He wants more football for his club, not less. Second-rate clubs will keep soccer in a second-rate situation.

KEITH BURKINSHAW, Spurs manager, **1982**.

WHAT hadn't been forseen was that when we broke up the television cartel, any loser in that cartel would turn round and try to break up the League.

GORDON TAYLOR, players' union secretary, on the ITV bid to sign up the 'Big Ten' clubs after the League reached agreement with British Satellite Broadcasting, **1988**.

WE are fully aware of what the consequences will be. What the League are offering is too little, too late.

MARTIN EDWARDS, Manchester United chairman, on the League's initial plan to forestall a breakaway Super League, **1988**.

WHAT has offended so many clubs is the feeling of betrayal, that the people we elected to safeguard the League's interests have been negotiating to leave the other 82 clubs in the lurch.

DEREK DOOLEY, Sheffield United managing director, **1988**.

IF we give in to them on this it will be the thin end of the wedge. They'll want freedom from relegation next and extra League points for being big clubs.

JOHN POYNTON, Coventry chairman, on the attempt by the 'Big Ten' clubs to do a unilateral deal with ITV, **1988**.

IT is an idea that smacks of Judas money, based on pure greed.

POYNTON, **1988**.

DAVID BULSTRODE: I think you will find, Gordon, that money talks.
GORDON TAYLOR: Let's wait and see how strong football's voice is.

EXCHANGE between the late QPR chairman and PFA secretary, **1988**.

PEOPLE say we're in a Wall Street game. In the League's centenary year, it's an absolute disgrace. They owe more than that to the sport.

GORDON TAYLOR, **1988**.

WE think club directors should be made to sit an exam and meet certain terms and conditions to prove their fitness to administer the game. They've harmed it just as much as the hooligans.

STEVE BEAUCHAMPÉ, Football Supporters' Association spokesman, **1988**.

OUR football belongs to the people – not to the property magnates and business tycoons who tried to hijack it for their own greedy interests.

JIMMY GREAVES on Super League plotting, **1988**.

WE negotiated a bonanza for the whole of the League, but football is now long on TV money and short on gratitude. What other business would want to get rid of you for making them £44m?

> DAVID DEIN, Arsenal vice-chairman, defending his place on the management committee, **1988**.

THAT'S not birdshit. That's Second Division chairmen for you.

> DEIN on being dumped upon by a pigeon after being removed from League management committee, **1988**.

IF I get on the management committee I'll fight like hell to maintain the Third and Fourth Divisions. I'm not interested in having a Super League. Our League is 92 clubs, and that's why it's the best.

> BOBBY CHARLTON, Manchester United director, **1988**.

Identity Cards

I hope she [Mrs Thatcher] is not going to be two-faced enough to turn up in the Royal Box at the next FA Cup Final, because she hasn't been football's friend.

> BRIAN CLOUGH on the Government response to the Heysel Stadium tragedy, after which ID cards were first mooted by the Prime Minister, **1985**.

IN sport, it would be nice if we could recover our reputation and in soccer once again become the gentleman of Europe.

> MRS THATCHER'S New Year message, **1988**.

THEY know on the Continent that European football without the English is like a hot dog without mustard.

> BOBBY CHARLTON, **1988**.

230 THE BOOK OF FOOTBALL QUOTATIONS

THE regrettable fact is that the FA and League have not warmly welcomed the initiative we have taken. I say to them, if they do not fast realize the lesson learnt at Luton Town [members-only club], then the Government will have to show them the way forward.

COLIN MOYNIHAN MP, Minister for Sport, in wake of fighting involving England fans at European Championships, **1988**.

THE Sports Minister is running round Germany like an interview waiting to happen.

BRIAN GLANVILLE, *Sunday Times*, on Moynihan's eagerness to give press conferences on England fans' behaviour, **1988**.

SMALL, but imperfectly informed.

GLANVILLE on the diminutive Moynihan, **1988**.

IT's all right for you, you won't need an ID card. You can always get in through the cat-flap.

DENNIS SKINNER MP to Moynihan, **1989**.

MEMBERSHIP schemes may work at some grounds, but I feel they are a nonsense. One end of the ground was half full and the other was packed to capacity. It is a well intentioned policy, but not right for London. It does not cater for transient supporters.

MET POLICE Chief Superintendent after QPR *v* West Ham game was delayed for an hour by fans spilling on to the pitch, **1988**.

WE believe this Bill will break the link between violence and soccer.

MOYNIHAN on Football Spectators Bill, which would make ID cards compulsory, **1988**. His colleagues Nicholas Ridley MP and Lord Caithness used the same phrase.

THE Prime Minister is talking about an industry of which she has no experience, and at the moment she is misguided.

GORDON TAYLOR, players' union secretary, **1988**.

IT wasn't a working party, it was a nodding dog party. Moynihan said, 'This is what 'er indoors wants' and they all nodded their heads in agreement.

ROGAN TAYLOR, chairman of Football Supporters' Association, **1988**.

ANYONE not prepared to carry such an identity card is up to no good or suffering from advanced libertarianism.

DR RHODES BOYSON MP, **1988**.

I don't know of anyone who is in favour of the scheme unless you happen to walk along Downing Street and bump into the Minister.

EDDIE PLUMLEY, chairman of League Executive Staff Association, **1988**.

UNTIL now [the thugs] have had to ask their victims: 'Are you one of us or one of them?' Now they'll just ask to see your ID card.

DENIS HOWELL MP, Shadow Minister for Sport, **1988**.

MRS Thatcher's Football (Suppression of Fans) Bill could leave a nasty taste in the mouth of the electorate. It is an ill-considered, petulant and petty measure, an exercise in prejudice and a fraud upon the citizen.

PETER JENKINS, political columnist, the *Independent*, **1989**.

IF you want to find hooliganism you don't go to the Kop, or the Den, or the Shed, you go to Bracknell or Windsor.

LORD GRAHAM OF EDMONTON in House of Lords debate, **1989**.

NEIL KINNOCK: Anybody who knows anything about football knows you are talking through the back of your neck.
MARGARET THATCHER: In talking through the back of the neck, I can't hold a candle to you.

EXCHANGE between Leader of Opposition and PM in Commons over Bill, **1989**.

COLIN MOYNIHAN: Why did you call me a twister?
DENIS HOWELL: Because I couldn't call you a little shit.

EXCHANGE between Minister and Shadow after Commons debate, **1989**.

I wish the Minister had been there to see the chaos.

MARTIN EDWARDS, Manchester United chief executive, after kick-off was delayed and 8000 fans locked out of FA Cup replay, **1989**.

THE accident-prone Football Spectators Bill reaches new heights of absurdity with the Government's insistence that women as well as men must carry ID cards not on the grounds of sex equality or because we have a problem with female hooligans, but because the blokes would otherwise squeeze themselves into mini-skirts, padded blouses and wigs, slosh on a bit of lipstick and totter off to the terraces on high heels.

That, at any rate, was how several of their Lordships took it when Lord Hesketh, Environment Under-Secretary, warned them of the lengths hooligans might go to to get into a match. 'I would remind your Lordships,' he cautioned them, 'of the Inter-City Firm whose speciality is to look quite unlike yobboes.'

I do not go to soccer matches but I think I would travel many miles to watch two rival gangs of hooligans in drag sloshing one another with their handbags.

KEITH WATERHOUSE, columnist, *Daily Mail*, **1989**.

MOYNIHAN is a very small spot on Arsenal defender Tony Adams's bottom. Albania is one of the most closed societies in the world, but next season it will be easier to watch a game there than in England.

ATTILA THE STOCKBROKER, poet-ranter, before Albania *v* England match, **1989**.

Hillsborough

THE FA Cup isn't worth it. There is nothing worth one death, let alone 100.

KENNY DALGLISH, Liverpool manager, after 95 fans were crushed to death during FA Cup semi-final *v* Nottingham Forest, **1989**.

NOTHING matters compared to what happened at Hillsborough.

PAT NEVIN, Everton match-winner at the other semi-final.

FOOTBALL is the one thing we did as a family and now we are not a family any more.

TREVOR HICKS, who tried in vain to save his two daughters with the 'kiss of life' at Sheffield.

THE police thought they were dealing with a security problem. It was comparatively late when they realised they had a major safety problem.

GRAHAM KELLY, FA secretary.

ONE had the impression they were beasts who wanted to charge into the arena. It was not far from hooliganism.

JACQUES GEORGE, president of UEFA.

HIS remarks showed he knew nothing of the events. He got it completely wrong.

DOUGLAS HURD MP, Home Secretary, on Monsieur George's comments.

THE ignorance and mischief-making from a rich and powerful Frenchman is beneath contempt. If he had an ounce of the humanity of most French people he would resign tomorrow and live a life of shame.

KEVA COOMBES, Leader of Liverpool City Council.

PERHAPS my words were too harsh.

JACQUES GEORGE.

MY flesh creeps today. I'm afraid Liverpool will always be stained by this double experience, different but somehow the same: Brussels and Sheffield. People will see them as the team of bloodshed and death at the stadium.

MICHEL PLATINI, a Juventus player at Heysel.

A whole culture of *en masse* support is coming to an end.

RICHARD FAULKNER, Director of the Football Trust.

I thought there were a number of officers who, whether because they were not directed, not inclined or did not know what to do, did nothing.

PC PETER GARRETT, Liverpool policeman and co-founder of Football Supporters Association, on his South Yorkshire colleagues.

AT last someone has acknowledged the existence of football supporters – after 100 years of being ignored.

ROGAN TAYLOR, FSA chairman, after Lord Justice Taylor's announcement that FSA would have equal status with FA, clubs and police at Hillsborough Inquiry.

THE Minister for Sport has responsibility for these things, for God's sake. There was no resuscitation equipment on the pitch and an oxygen cylinder was empty. Let the supporters organize matches in future. They would do it better.

DR GLYNN PHILIPS, spectator who tended the injured and dying.

THE saddest and most beautiful sight I've ever seen.

KENNY DALGLISH on tribute of flowers and scarves at Anfield.

13
Literary Lions and Cup Vinylists

THE sturdie ploughman, lustie, strong and bold,
Overcometh the winter with driving the foote-ball,
Forgetting labour and many a grievous fall.

ALEXANDER BARCLAY in *Fifth Eclogue*, **1508**.

THE streets were full of footballs.

SAMUEL PEPYS in his diary, 2 January, **1665**.

AM I so round with you as you with me.
That like a football you do spurn me thus?
You spurn me hence, and he will spurn me hither;
If I last in this service you must case me in leather.

WILLIAM SHAKESPEARE in *Comedy of Errors*, **1590**.

OSWALD: I'll not be strucken, my lord.
KENT: Nor tripp'd neither, you base football player. (*Tripping up his heels*).

SHAKESPEARE in *King Lear*, **1608**.

ANTHONY: Do we have best them to their beds. What, girl! though grey
 Do something mingle with our younger brown, yet ha'we
 A brain that nourishes our nerves, and can
 Get goal for goal of youth.

SHAKESPEARE in *Antony and Cleopatra*, **1608**.

LIKE a wild Irish, I'll nere thinke thee dead.
Till I can play at football with thy head.

JOHN WEBSTER in *The White Devil*, **1612**.

How the quoit
Wizz'd from the stripling's arm!
If touched by him,
The inglorious football mounted to the pitch
Of the lark's flight, – or shaped a rainbow curve
Aloft, in prospect of the shouting field.

WILLIAM WORDSWORTH in *The Excursion*, **1814**.

THEN strip lads and to it, though sharp be the weather
And if, by mischance, you should happen to fall,
There are worse things in life than a tumble in the heather,
And life itself is but a game of football.

SIR WALTER SCOTT, on the occasion of a match between Ettrick and Selkirk, **1815**.

TWICE a week the winter through
Here stood I to keep the goal:
Football then was fighting sorrow
For the young man's soul.

A. E. HOUSMAN, *A Shropshire Lad*, **1896**.

THEN ye returned to your trinkets;
Then ye contented your souls
With the flanelled fools at the wicket
Or the muddied oafs at the goals.

RUDYARD KIPLING in *The Islanders*, **1902**.

FOOTBALL is all very well as a game for rough girls, but it is hardly
suitable for delicate boys.

OSCAR WILDE.

'BUT I don't see what football has got to do with being mayor.' She endeavoured to look like a serious politician. 'You are nothing but a cuckoo,' Denry pleasantly informed her. 'Football has got to do with everything.'

ARNOLD BENNETT in *The Card*, **1911**.

'I'VE lost that £2000 in thirteen years. That is, it's the same as if I'd been steadily paying three pun' a week out of my own pocket to provide football matches that you chaps wouldn't take the trouble to go and see. That's the straight of it! What have I got for my pains? Nothing but worries and these!' (He pointed to his grey hairs). . . . 'Me and my co-directors,' he proceeded, with even tougher raspishness, 'have warned the town again and again what would happen if the matches weren't better patronized. And now it's happening, and now it's too late, you want to *do* something! You can't! It's too late. There's only one thing the matter with first-class football in Bursley,' he concluded, 'and it isn't the players. It's the public – it's yourselves. You're the most craven lot of tom-fools that ever a big football club had to do with.'

ARNOLD BENNETT, as above.

RANGERS would play with the sou'westerly wind, straight towards the goal behind which Danny stood in eagerness. This was enough to send a man off his head. Good old Rangers – and to hell with the Pope.

GEORGE BLAKE in *The Shipbuilders*, **1957**.

NEARLY two hours thereafter Danny Shields lived far beyond himself in a whirling world of passion. Not a man on the terrace paused to reflect that it was a spectacle cunningly arranged to draw their shillings or to remember that the twenty-two players were so many slaves of a commercial system, liable to be bought and sold like fallen women without any regard to their feelings as men. The men on the terraces found release from the drabness of their own industrial degradation.

GEORGE BLAKE, as above.

To say that these men paid their shillings to watch twenty-two hirelings kick a ball is merely to say that a violin is wood and catgut, that Hamlet is so much paper and ink. For a shilling the Bruddersford United AFC offered you Conflict and Art . . .

J. B. PRIESTLEY in *The Good Companions*, **1929**.

A man who had missed the last home match of 't 'United' had to enter social life on tiptoe in Bruddersford.

J. B. PRIESTLEY, as above.

IT turned you into a member of a community, all brothers together for an hour and a half, for not only had you escaped from the clanking machinery of the lesser life, from work, wages, rent, doles, sick pay, insurance cards, nagging wives, ailing children, bad bosses, idle workmen, but you had escaped with most of your mates, and your neighbours, with half the town, and there you were, cheering together, thumping one another on the shoulders, swapping judgements like lords of the earth, having punched your way through a turnstile into another and altogether more special kind of life.

J. B. PRIESTLEY, as above.

'No, no,' said Pnin, 'do not wish an egg, or, for example, a torpedo. I want a simple football. Round!'

VLADIMIR NABOKOV, *Pnin*, **1957**.

GUS: I saw the Villa get beat in a Cup tie once. Who was it against now? White shirts. It was one-all at half-time. I'll never forget it. Their opponents won by a penalty. Talk about drama. Yes, it was a disputed penalty. Disputed. They got beat two-one, anyway, because of it. You were there yourself.
BEN: Not me.
GUS: Yes, you were there. Don't you remember that disputed penalty?
BEN: No.
GUS: He went down just inside the area. They said he was just acting. I didn't think the other bloke touched him myself. But the referee had the ball on the spot.

BEN: Didn't touch him! What are you talking about? He laid him out flat!

GUS: Not the Villa. The Villa don't play that sort of game.

HAROLD PINTER, *The Dumb Waiter*, **1960**.

THE clean programmes are trampled underfoot,
and natural the dark, appropriate the rain,
whilst, under lamp posts, threatening newsboys shout.

DANNIE ABSE, from 'The Game', **1962**.

AND that, boys, is how to take a penalty. Look one way, and kick to the other.

SUGDEN, the games teacher (played by Brian Glover) in film *Kes*, scripted by Barry Hines, **1969**.

I could've been a footballer, but I had a paper round.

YOSSER HUGHES, played by Bernard Hill, in *Boys from the Blackstuff*, scripted by Alan Bleasdale, **1981**.

HEADMASTER: I see as usual our effort was spoilt by the vociferous minority. The gang who only feel something when they have a red and white scarf round their necks. The people who are only brave in a 50,000 crowd. The people who have got nothing out of school life, and put nothing in. The people who think all the world's a football pitch. For the rest of us, there are more things in life than football.

PETER TERSON, *Zigger Zagger*, **1967**. Hymns in school assembly had been disrupted by chants of 'City!'

THE old architecture of soccer, the grim shabbiness of the corrugated iron age, had gone now. Where once there had been one upright stand and three sides of uncovered, weed-threatened terraces, there were now massive cantilever stands on three sides of the arena, their apparently unsupported roofs jutting dramatically into the blue sky like the dark dorsal fins of monstrous sharks.

GORDON WILLIAMS & TERRY VENABLES, *They Used to Play on Grass*, **1971**.

TODAY even the grass had gone. Commoners had been one of the last clubs in the First Division to install the new plastic turf. In the summer they had dug up the old grass pitch and replaced it with new man made wonder stuff, bright green and totally dead. They had sold off the old pitch at twenty shillings a square foot. People had formed queues to buy a slice of sentimental sod.

WILLIAMS & VENABLES, as above.

FROM . . . sunrise until it became too dark to see in the evening, the steady thump-thump of a boot on a ball could be heard somewhere in the barracks. It was tolerated because there was no alternative; even the parade ground was not sacred from the small, shuffling figures of the Glasgow men, their bonnets pulled down over their eyes, kicking, trapping, swerving and passing, and occasionally intoning, like ugly little high priests, their ritual cries of 'Way-ull' and 'Aw-hay-hey'. The simile is apt, for it was almost a religious exercise, to be interrupted only if the Colonel happened to stroll by.

GEORGE MACDONALD FRASER, 'Play Up, Play Up and Get Tore In' from *The General Danced At Dawn*, **1970**.

I used to watch them wheeling like gulls, absorbed in their wonderful fitba'. They weren't in Africa or the Army any longer; in imagination they were running on the green turf of Ibrox or Paradise, hearing instead of bugle calls the rumble and roar of a hundred thousand voices; this was their common daydream, to play (according to religion) either for Celtic or Rangers. All except Daft Bob Brown, the battalion idiot; in his fantasy he was playing for Partick Thistle.

GEORGE MACDONALD FRASER, as above.

I'M a schizofanatic, sad burrits true
One half of me's red, and the other half's blue.
I can't make up me mind which team to support
Whether to lean to starboard or port
I'd be bisexual if I had time for sex
Cos it's Goodison one week and Anfield the next.

ROGER MCGOUGH in 'Footy Poem', **1975**.

GRAYSON: Make no mistake, comma, the four-goal credit which these slick Slovaks netted here this afternoon will keep them in the black through the second leg of the World Cup eliminator at Wembley next month, stop. New par.

CHAMBERLAIN: Wilson, who would like to be thought the big bad man of the England defence, merely looked slow-footed and slow-witted, stop. Deml – D.E.M. mother L. – Deml got round him five times on the trot, bracket, literally, close bracket, using the same swerve, comma, making Wilson look elephantine in everything but memory, stop.

TOM STOPPARD in the television play *Professional Foul*, **1977**. The two reporters are filing copy from a hotel in Prague.

. . . AT least he no longer maintained that Nature belonged exclusively to the Gentiles. Football, however – he continued to maintain – did. And he was not merely thinking of the obvious ways in which the game was not Jewish; that it owed its origins to a working-class culture that was shaped when the Jews were elsewhere; that it was played on Saturdays – the day of rest; that it was a violent game demanding of its players sinew and brawn, whereas Jewish men had soft skin and bruised easily. This last was no small consideration. The whole art of existence, for many a Jew of Sefton's acquaintance, was to avoid sedulously, in one lifetime, the brutality of conflict and collision that the average footballer enjoyed in an hour and a half.

HOWARD JACOBSON, *Coming from Behind*, **1983**.

SUCH fears were alien to football. Above all else, the game gloried in the passing, delirious moment; gave the illusory promise, to players and spectators, of irreversible triumph and permanent reward. The scorer of the goal taunted the opposition, jeered at detractors in the crowd, lifted his fists to the heavens, unable to prefigure, though it happened every week, that a moment later his team would be the object of identical mockery and he would have to show his dejection as shamelessly as he had shown his delight. It was the unimaginativeness of irreligion; the optimism of impiety.

JACOBSON, as above.

A Jewish team unfortunate enough to take an early lead would have kept it quiet and hoped that no-one noticed.

JACOBSON, as above.

Sefton stood dispiritedly at the window of his room and looked out across the flattened town to the sloping, rusting, corrugated roof of Wrottesley Ramblers Football Club. His new Academic home! He did not want to go there. . . . If he was going to spend the rest of his days in a football stand he might as well have played rough games in the school playground. . . . And acquired some skills more appropriate to his future style of life: how to squirm under a turnstile, which part of the forehead to use when nutting a policeman.

JACOBSON, as above.

What everyone was invited to was the Official twinning of Wrottesley Polytechnic with Wrottesley Ramblers, to be held in the presence of his worshipful the Mayor, on a date which Sefton calculated to be only a little over a fortnight from today. . . .
    'This is actually to take place in the stadium?' he checked, unexceptionably curious.
    'Before the fans, yes. It should be a capacity crowd.'
    'I thought attendances were quite low over there at the moment.'
    'They'll be playing Manchester United on that day.'
    'I see,' said Sefton. . . . 'So it should be good for recruitment?'
    'Exactly. That's Sidewinder's plan. Take the Polytechnic to the people.'

JACOBSON, as above.

'Me, I had to start with rubbish. I've done miracles with rubbish. Worked wonders with rubbish. I knew about recycling before it had ever been invented. But you get no medals for that.'
    And he hadn't. He'd last three months here, six months there, then something would snap, he'd quarrel with the chairman, blow his top to the press, even thump one of the players, and out he'd go, off we'd go; another little house, poor Mother packing and unpacking all over again.

BRIAN GLANVILLE, short story Love is not Love, 1985.

The scruffiest long-haired layabouts I have ever seen assembled in one place since Nouvian were at home to Port Vale in a pre-war friendly. A complete shower, a shambles.

THE WAR DIARIES OF RENÉ ARTOIS, literary spin-off from BBC TV's 'Allo, 'Allo', on Italian troops, 1988.

'I may be going on t'transfer list,' said Tommy. 'You'll be t'first to know if I do.'

'Leave Thurmarsh?' said Henry.

'Can Muir and Ayers give me the through-balls I need if I'm to utilize my speed? Can they buggery! I've got the scoring instincts of a predatory panther, and I'm being sacrificed on the altar of mid-table mediocrity.'

'You've been reading too many press reports.'

'You what?'

DAVID NOBBS, *Pratt of the Argus*, **1988**.

'WHAT about loyalty to the team that made you?' said Henry. 'What about loyalty to the town that took an urchin off the streets and turned him into a star?'

'You've been reading too many press reports,' said Tommy. 'Listen. Only last night I heard about one of t'directors, who's buying up half t'town centre dirt cheap so he can redevelop it at vast profits. Loyalty to Thurmarsh? Don't make me laugh.'

'Which director?' said Henry.

'I've told you too much already,' said Tommy.

NOBBS, as above.

PAUL shook his head in amazement at the latest eccentricity of his funny little northern friend, and they entered Twickenham, known the world over as Twickers. Henry felt that he ought to be watching Thurmarsh play Rochdale at Blonk Lane, known nowhere as Blonkers.

NOBBS, as above.

THIS graveyard on the brink of Beeston Hill's
The place I may well rest if there's a spot
under the rose roots and the daffodils
by which dad dignified the family plot.

If buried ashes saw then I'd survey
the places I learned Latin, and learned Greek,
and left, the ground where Leeds United play
but disappoint their fans week after week,

which makes them lose their sense of self-esteem
and taking a short cut home through these graves here
they reassert the glory of their team
by spraying words on tombstones, pissed on beer.

TONY HARRISON, from *V.*, **1985**.

HE's fitba' crazy, he's fitba' mad
And the fitba' it has robbed him o' the wee bit sense he had
And it would take a dozen skivvies his claes to wash and scrub
Since oor Jock became a member of that terrible fitba' club.

ROBIN HALL and JIMMY MACGREGOR record, 'Football Crazy', **1960**.

OSSIE's going to Wembley.
His knees have gone all trembly.

SPURS' FA Cup final record, **1981**.

IF Inglan want to do some good
Hear me now, hear me Ron Greenwood
Put away your pride and prejudice
And carry the man Cyrille Regis

DENNIS ALCAPONE, reggae single 'World Cup Football', **1982**.

WHY don't Rangers sign a Catholic?

4 BE 2s' song title, **1983**.

ALL I want for Christmas is a Dukla Prague away strip.

HALF MAN HALF BISCUIT record title on joys of Subbuteo, **1986**.

SOME people are on the pitch they think it's all over it is now.

THE DENTISTS' LP title, **1986**.

RUCKING in the terrace
Bundles in the seats
Fighting for glory in half-lit streets
Say they're gonna stop us
Won't let us go
But they'll never get us
On video.

THE BUSINESS on single, 'Saturday's Heroes', **1988**.

MOYNIHAN (Brings Out the Hooligan in Me).

I, LUDICROUS, song title from LP compilation of anti-ID card songs, **1989**.

BILLY Bonds MBE.

BARMY ARMY flexi-disc title, **1988**.

I Was A Teenage Armchair Honved Fan.

HALF MAN HALF BISCUIT song title, **1986**.

HE always beat me at Subbuteo
Cos he flicked to kick
And I didn't know

THE UNDERTONES, from single 'My Perfect Cousin', **1981**. Group also recorded 'When Saturday Comes', whose title became the name of a football magazine.

Y Viva El Fulham.

TONY REES & THE COTTAGERS' single title, **1975**.

OH! We're off to Munich for the Cup
Viva the Jambos
No they can't deflate us when we're up
Viva the Jambos
When our boys confuse them on the wing
Dancing their samba
You will hear the fans behind them sing
'Oh Jambos score one more'

HEART OF MIDLOTHIAN Executive Club souvenir songbook, **1989**. 'Jambos' comes from 'Jam Tarts', rhyming slang for Hearts.

I come from Jamaica
My name is John Barn-es
When I do my thing
The crowd go bananas!

JOHN BARNES on Liverpool single, 'Anfield Rap', **1988**.

How can you lie back and think of England
When you don't even know who's in the team

BILLY BRAGG on single, 'Greetings to the New Brunette', **1986.**

Bibliography

A Little Thing called Pride, Alec Stock, (Pelham, 1982)
A Red Dragon of Wales, Roy Paul, (Robert Hale 1956)
The All American War Game, James Lawton, (Basil Blackwell, 1984)
All for the Wolves, Stan Cullis, (Hart-Davis 1960)
An Autobiography, Denis Law, (Queen Anne Press, 1979)
Sir Alf Ramsey, Anatomy of a Football Manager, Max Marquis, (Arthur Barker, 1970)
Anatomy of a Football Star: George Best, David Meek, (Arther Barker, 1970)
Another Breath of Fred Eyre, Fred Eyre, (Senior Publications, 1982)
Arsenal from the Heart, Bob Wall, (Souvenir Press, 1969)
Association Football and the Men who made it, William Pickford and Alfred Gibson (Caxton Publishing Company, 1906)
At Home with the Hammers, Ted Fenton, (Nicholas Kaye, 1960)
Attack from the Back, Phil Neal, (Arthur Barker, 1981)
Barnsley – A Study in Football 1953–39, Ian Allister and Andrew Ward, (Crowberry, 1981)
Blackpool Football, Robin Daniels, (Robert Hale, 1972)
The Book of Football, William Isiah Barrett, (1906)
The Boys in Maroon, John Fairgrieve, (Mainstream Publishing, 1986)
Boys of '66, Martin Tyler, (Hamlyn, 1981)
Boys Own Annual, 1933–34, 1936–37 (R.T.S. Lutterworth Press)
Both Sides of the Border, Terry Butcher, (Arthur Barker, 1987)
Bristol Rovers, A complete record 1883–1987: Mike Jay (Breedon Books, 1987)
Call the Doc, Tommy Docherty, (Hamlyn, 1981)
Captain of England, Billy Wright, (Stanley Paul, 1950)
Captain of Hungary, Ferenc Puskas, (Cassell, 1955)
The Card, Arnold Bennett, (Methuen, 1911)
Celtic Greats, Hugh Keevins, (John Donald, 1988)
Cliff Bastin Remembers, Cliff Bastin, (Ettrick Press, 1950)
Colours of My Life, Malcolm Allison, (Everest, 1975)
Coming from Behind, Howard Jacobson, (Chatto & Windus/The Hogarth Edition, 1983)
Concerning Soccer, John Arlott, (Longmans Green, 1952)
Corinthians, Casuals and Cricketers, Edward Grayson, (Naldrett Press, 1955)
The Derby County Story, Andrew Ward and Anton Rippon, (Breedon Books, 1983)
Diaries of a Cabinet Minister 1964–70, Richard Crossman MP, (Cape/Hamilton, 1979)
Diary of a Season, Lawrie McMenemy, (Arthur Barker, 1979)
The Dumb Waiter, Harold Pinter, (Samuel French., acting edt. 1961)
The Encyclopedia of Association Football, Edited by Geoffrey Green, (Caxton 1960)

The European Cup 1955–80, John Motson and John Rowlinson, (Queen Anne Press, 1980)
FA Book of Soccer, (Pan Books, 1975)
Father of Football, David Miller, (Stanley Paul, 1970)
Fifty Years of Football, Sir Frederick Wall, (Cassell, 1935)
Finney on Football, Tom Finney, (Nicholas Kaye, 1958)
Football as a Profession, Derek Dougan and Dr Percy M. Young, (Stanley Paul, 1974)
Football Hooliganism, The Wider Context, Roger Ingham, (Inter-Action, 1978)
Football is My Passport, Billy Wright, (Stanley Paul, 1957)
The Football Man, Arthur Hopcraft, (Collins, 1968)
The Football Managers, Tony Pawson, (Eyre Methuen, 1973)
Football Worlds – A Lifetime in Sport, Sir Stanley Rous, (Faber, 1978)
Football with the Millionaires, Eddie Firmani, (Stanley Paul, 1959)
Football Year, Dr Percy M. Young, (Phoenix House, 1956)
Forward Arsenal, Bernard Joy, (Phoenix House, 1952)
The Game, Dannie Abse, (1962)
The General Danced at Dawn, George Macdonald Fraser, (Barrie & Jenkins, 1970)
The Gentle Giant, John Charles, (Stanley Paul, 1962)
Give a Little Whistle, Gordon Hill, (Souvenir Press, 1975)
The Good Companions, J.B. Priestley, (Heinemann, 1929)
Goodbye to Yorkshire, Roy Hattersley MP, (Penguin, 1976)
The Great Derbies, Everton v Liverpool, Brian Barwick and Gerald Sinstadt, (BBC, 1988)
Great Masters of Scottish Football, Hugh Taylor, (Stanley Paul, 1967/8)
Hardaker of the League, Alan Hardaker, (Pelham, 1977)
A History of Chelsea FC, Ralph L Finn, (Pelham Books, 1969)
The History of the World Cup, Brian Glanville, (Faber and Faber, 1980)
Howard Kendall's Everton Scrapbook, (Souvenir Press, 1986)
I Don't Bruise Easily, Brian Close, (Macdonald & Jane's, 1978)
Inside Soccer, Tony Woodcock, (Queen Anne Press, 1985)
Jock Stein – The Authorized Biography, Ken Gallacher, (Stanley Paul, 1988)
Journey to Wembley, Brian James, (Marshall Cavendish, 1977)
Jousting with Giants, Jim McLean, (Mainstream Publishing, 1987)
Love is not Love, Brian Glanville, (Anthony Blond, 1985)
Peter Shilton: The Magnificent Obsession, Jason Tomas, (World's Work, 1982)
A Man for all Seasons, Steve Perryman, (Arthur Barker, 1985)
Memoirs and Observations of M. Misson in his travels over England, J. Misson (1967)
Mexico 70, Martin Peters (Cassell, 1970)
Mo, Maurice Johnston, (Mainstream Publishing, 1988)
My Fight for Football, Bob Lord, (Stanley Paul, 1963)
My Soccer Story, Billy Liddell, (Stanley Paul, 1960)
My Story, Matt Busby, (Souvenir Press, 1957)
No Half Measures, Graeme Souness, (Collins, 1985)
No Half Measures, Graeme Souness, (Grafton Books, 1987)
Oh, Ref!, Pat Partridge, (Souvenir Press, 1979)
One Hundred Years of Scottish Football, John Rafferty, (Pan, 1973)
100 Great British Footballers, Trevor Brooking, (Queen Anne Press, 1980)
Only a Game?, Eamon Dunphy, (Kestrel, 1976)
Pele! My Life and the Beautiful Game, Pele with Robert L. Fish (Doubleday & Co. Inc., USA, 1977) (New English Library UK, 1977)
Pnin, Vladimir Nabokov, (Heinemann, 1957)
Pompey's Gentleman Jim, Peter Jeffs, (Breedon Books, 1988)
Pratt of the Argus, David Nobbs, (Methuen London Ltd, 1988)

The Pursuit of Sporting Excellence, David Hemery, (Collins Willow, 1986)
Right Inside Soccer, Jimmy McIlroy, (Nicholas Kaye, 1960)
Rothman's Football Yearbook 1979–80 (Queen Anne Press, 1979)
Shades of Gray, Andy Gray, (Queen Anne Press, 1986)
The Shipbuilders, George Blake, (Collins, 1957)
Soccer at Home and Abroad, Neil Franklin (Stanley Paul, 1956)
Soccer Choice, Bryon Butler and Ron Greenwood, (Pelham, 1979)
Soccer's Happy Wanderer, Don Revie, (Museum Press, 1955)
Soccer the British Way, Joe Mercer, (Nicholas Kaye, 1963)
Soccer: The Road to Crisis, Anton Rippon, (Moorland Publishing Co, 1983)
Sportsmen of Cornwall, Michael George, (Bossiney Books, Bodmin, 1986)
Spurs – The Double, Julian Holland, (Heinemann, 1961)
The Stanley Matthews Story, Stanley Matthews, (Oldbourne, 1960)
Striking for Soccer, Jimmy Hill, (Peter Davies, 1961)
There's only one Clive Allen, Clive Allen, (Arthur Barker, 1987)
This One's on Me, Jimmy Greaves, (Arthur Barker, 1979)
They used to Play on Grass, Gordon Williams and Terry Venables, (Hodder & Stroughton, 1971)
Time on the Grass, Bobby Robson, (Arthur Barker, 1982)
Tom Whittaker's Arsenal Story, Tom Whittaker, (Sporting Handbooks, 1957)
V, Tony Harrison, (Bloodaxe Books, 1986)
Viv Anderson Autobiography, Viv Anderson, (Kingswood, 1988)
The War Diaries of Rene Artois, John Haselden, (BBC, 1988)
We'll Support you ever more, John Rafferty, (1976)
When will we see Your Like Again? Edited by Mike Aitken, (EUSPB Edinburgh, 1977)
With Clough by Taylor, Peter Taylor, (Sidgwick and Jackson, 1980)
World Cup: The Argentina Story, David Miller, (Frederick Warne, 1978)
World Soccer Referee, Jack Taylor, (Pelham, 1976)
You Get Nowt for Coming Second, Billy Bremner, (Souvenir Press Ltd, 1969)

Photograph Acknowledgements

The authors and publishers are grateful to the following for allowing use of copyright photographs:

AllSport, Shankly gates; BBC Picture Publicity, Kenneth Wolstenholme and Alexei Sayle; Colorsport, Charlie Nicholas, Vinny Jones with FA cup medal, Bryan Robson, Brian Clough, Erik Thorstvedt, Trevor Peake and Clive Allen, Crystal Palace celebrating a goal, George Best; the *Guardian,* inflatable whales; the *Independent,* derelict Valley ground, England fans' T-shirt, Steve Bull; London News Service, Vinny Jones and Paul Gascoigne; Press Association, Roy of the Rovers, Malcolm Allison; Syndication International, Billy Bremner, Jack Charlton; Bob Thomas, John Barnes.

Index